Yo Soy

Yo Soy

From a Migrant Field Worker to a University Professor

Roberto E. Villarreal

Number 14 in the Al Filo, Mexican American Studies Series

UNT PRESS

University of North Texas Press
Denton, Texas

Printed in the United States of America.

10 9 8 7 6 5 4 3 2 1

Permissions:
University of North Texas Press
1155 Union Circle #311336
Denton, TX 76203-5017

The paper used in this book meets the minimum requirements of the American National Standard for Permanence of Paper for Printed Library Materials, z39.48.1984. Binding materials have been chosen for durability.

Library of Congress Cataloging-in-Publication Data

Names: Villarreal, Roberto E. author
Title: Yo Soy : from a migrant field worker to a university professor / Roberto E. Villarreal.
Other titles: Al filo no. 14.
Description: Denton : University of North Texas Press, [2025] | Series: Al filo, Mexican American studies series ; Number 14 | Includes bibliographical references and index.
Identifiers: LCCN 2025043656 (print) | LCCN 2025043657 (ebook) | ISBN 9781574419856 cloth | ISBN 9781574419931 ebook
Subjects: LCSH: Villarreal, Roberto E. | University of Texas at El Paso--Faculty--Biography | Political scientists--Texas--El Paso--Biography | Mexican American college teachers--Texas--El Paso--Biography | College teachers--Texas--El Paso--Biography | Mexican American college administrators--Texas--El Paso--Biography | College administrators--Texas--El Paso--Biography | Mexican American civic leaders--Texas--El Paso--Biography | Civic leaders--Texas--El Paso--Biography | Mexican American migrant agricultural laborers--United States--Biography | Mexican Americans--Education (Higher) | Hispanic Americans--Education | LCGFT: Autobiographies
Classification: LCC JC274.5.V55 A3 2025 (print) | LCC JC274.5.V55 (ebook)
LC record available at https://lccn.loc.gov/2025043656
LC ebook record available at https://lccn.loc.gov/2025043657

Yo Soy is Number 14 in the Al Filo, Mexican American Studies Series.

The electronic edition of this book was made possible by the support of the Vick Family Foundation.

Typeset by vPrompt eServices

Para Mis Padres,
Maria Antonia Escamilla Villarreal and
Epifanio Santos Villarreal Sr.,
who sacrificed their lives and fought incredibly
hard to make us who we are now,
and to my wife,
Norma Pedraza Villarreal,
who formed a trio with my parents to make
me what I am (*Yo Soy*).
Gracias!

“The roots of education are bitter,
but the fruit is sweet.”

—Aristotle

Contents

Preface

Why *Yo Soy* as a title for this memoir (*memorias*)? In this narrative I become the spokesman. But I am the spokesman for many people; I represent the beliefs and thoughts of many people, from both yesteryear and today. It means that when we face the world, we stand up to many obstacles; we are the people that raise our chins and pound our chest to claim what is right; and we stand up against segregation, discrimination, and subordination to reach for equality and social justice. That being said, my goal in this story is for the reader, especially the young reader, to know how different public education and the Mexican American family was two generations ago. This is a multigenerational epic. This story portrays the many struggles of prior generations to reach where we are now and, hopefully, give us newer directions to obtain full equality and justice. To accomplish this mission, I concentrate on my generation's efforts in higher education with the support of our ancestors and the community to transform the educational system to what it is now. The enemy of our struggle was a system partial to one group against the other. Sadly, it has been Anglos versus Mexican Americans. My generation was the first to attend universities, graduate, and then become part of the universities. Based on our experiences, we fought for our existence and the existence of others to overcome the injustices of a school system flawed with prejudices and biases against who we are. In this document I have been able to gather and categorize significant information in chronological order. My goal is that by the end of reading this volume, you will have a better portrayal of what has happened and what the future will be for years to come. Finally, throughout this memoir I make references to a survey that I conducted of "First Generation of Latinos in Higher Education" where Latinos entered and stayed in higher education from the early 1960s into the 1970s and 1980s.[1]

I have used a variety of terms to define the common names of groups that appear in this manuscript: *people of Mexican origin* (Mexicans from Mexico) *Hispanic, Hispano, Latina, Latino, Chicano, Mexican American,* and *Tejano*. These identifying terms are used interchangeably. Why? Because this growing and sizeable group classifies themselves in so many ways. To use one or two identities for all of them would be unfair. The same applies to the usage of the words *Anglo* and *white*. It is understood that there are differences in definition depending on the place and time. After serious consideration I have concluded that the interchangeability of these terms is proper for this memoir.

I was born in the 1930s in a community mainly of people of Mexican origin who were poverty stricken—sharecroppers and migrants. Like my siblings, I attended segregated schools. As migrants we traveled during the fall season, going from place to place, seeking work to survive. This took us away from school for a whole semester every year. Neither my parents, my siblings, nor I knew the English language. There was a complete disconnect between the Mexican American family and the public schools. Moreover, the culture of the school was drastically different from the culture of the Mexican American family.

All six of my siblings became dropouts before finishing fifth grade. This was typical in South Texas. Based on these circumstances, my future in education was in jeopardy. Still, I had two things in my favor. I was the *coyote* (youngest) of the family, and I was exceedingly stubborn. I flunked four times, not graduating from high school until the age of 22. These were some of the conditions that many of us had to face. Overcoming these troubles prepared me for the rest of my life to challenge the world. My hope is that you will navigate throughout these chapters to discover what humans can do when they believe in their dreams. This is a story with all possible dimensions that life brings to us: love, struggle, disappointment, frustration, humor, achievement, and many others.

Chapter 1

The Formative Years

This is a narrative of struggles and events that formed the foundation of my early years at a time when immigrant parents that came to the United States endured excessive hardships to raise a family in a world unknown to them. Ever since childhood I have had a sense of urgency of doing something to gradually change things, not knowing how or having power to do it. Short of vision and understanding, something was telling me that I had to reach out and make my parents proud of their sacrifices. Their struggles and disadvantages became part of my world. Although the trail that I was following lacked clarity and direction, the dream never left me. As I matured my commitment strengthened in the hopes of seeing light at the end of the tunnel and reaching the unreachable dream not only for me but also for my parents and *nuestra gente* (our people). This story unfolds in the next chapters.

This account includes many people who shouldered responsibility to make my dream a reality. Without these people I would never have written the story that I am writing today. This include my parents and family; the public school that, for all its problems and difficulties, ultimately got me through; the university that enlightened my scope and vision; a blind old man who taught me how to read and write Spanish; Anglos who understood minorities and were willing to stand up for what was right; and many more who took the risk of changing what needed to be done.

During my childhood the struggle to overcome subordination had no end in sight. A traditional agricultural economy gave us little opportunity to advance, and the domination of Anglos was devastating. We had a school system that was not responsive to people of Mexican origin, and parental participation at school was totally unknown. David Montejano, in his seminal book, *Anglos and Mexican Americans*, claimed that the most distinguished feature in the history of Texas is the sharp division between Anglos and Mexican Americans in our schools and everywhere else.[1]

This story is about the enormous struggles against social, political, cultural, economic, and environmental injustices. The arrivals of white Southerners to Texas back in the 1820s and thereafter did not serve Mexicans well. One of the reasons why it became destructive to Mexicans was the Anglo promotion of slavery since it was profitable. Over the years the slavery issue expanded, and Mexicans were in their path. Moving forward, when my generation came in the 1930s and 1940s, the world in South Texas was turned upside down. By this time Anglos were powerful and in full control. Discrimination and segregation were well established. The subordination of the Mexican Americans was complete.

That being said, Mexican American leaders knew that to remove this cloud, it would take newer avenues to find solutions. One of the critical avenues was how to resolve major issues with the school system since attending public schools was required. Moreover, we needed to learn the English language, and it was most desirable to integrate into the dominant culture. This was the way to be rewarded and have less pain. We understood that the cultural ramifications of the American system were central to our own welfare. There was a price to be paid for all these changes, and one of the major components of this price was our cultural heritage and language. At the same time, we would continue to cultivate our Mexican roots and culture. We have had the opportunity to become bilingual and bicultural, which is an enormous strength. Spanish people became the product of branches of a variation of cultures, starting with Native Americans, who undoubtedly have contributed immensely to our culture—far more than we ever give them credit for.

Spanish culture, with many adaptations from Mediterranean cultures, including Jews, combined with our mestizo heritage, form the foundation to operate in this hemisphere. In a study by Carrie Gibson, *El Norte: The Epic and Forgotten Story of Hispanic North America*, the author provides a powerful and genuine history where she characterizes the contributions of Hispanic people to the North American continent. In her classic work, she quotes Walt Whitman, considered as one of the most influential poets in American literature by saying that "Spanish character will supply some of the most need parts to understand our heritage."[2] Yet for more than 150 years we have not known the story of Hispanics in North America. To the contrary, for many years most Anglos have considered our culture and heritage inferior.

I grew up in rural South Texas surrounded by a large and extended family. Our family included relatives from Mexico who came to work and send money back home in order for the rest of the family to survive. The challenges before us were enormous, and our paths were unclear; we suffered greatly for not being organized, but how could we be organized living in rural areas and isolated from society? Quietly and individually we fought subordination and discrimination. The struggle to survive, particularly in my early years of public education, proved to be vastly difficult. I had to find a link to connect two separate worlds—school and family. Our parents never made any contact with the school system, nor did the school system make contact with Mexican American families. Fortunately, a few of us were able to bridge the gap between these two institutions.

For a family of sharecroppers, money was hard to come by. Although we had no debts, there were also no savings to maintain the family for the fall and winter months every year. Jobs for Mexican Americans were not available in town or anywhere else. We had one alternative: to move north to find jobs picking cotton. Preparations were made to migrate north as soon as the harvest season was over in South Texas. It did not matter if it we were at home or migrating; economically, my parents kept a very tight budget. The whole family worked for a common cause. None of us were paid or had an allowance; this was not part of our culture. Frankly, I did not know the meaning of the word *allowance*, nor did I know that it existed until I acquired middle-class values. Having allowances and vacations was unheard of in our circles. Dad and Mom would collect all the income and make all the financial decisions. From that financial center, a distribution was made to every member of the family. I have no idea how the distribution of coins was made or if older members of the family got more than others. All I knew was that my father and mother were doing their best to keep us afloat, and afloat we were.

Our ancestors in this region were tough, active, and resilient, and they had the determination to prevail, *pase lo que pase* (whatever happens). Our ancestors formed a verbally expressive community, a community that was practical and self-educated. In the early years, little was written about the culture and language of people of Mexican origin. Writings often fail to understand our culture, traditions, and history, and this has occurred from the top down, so many contributions have been forgotten. But in recent years, hundreds of academic books have been written, and the number of publications continues to grow. Yet in rural areas of South Texas, it has taken longer to catch up with these literary works. As noted in the bibliography of this study, recent books have provided a newer interpretation of our past. At a four-year reunion in Pawnee, where I went to high school, part of the celebration was a presentation by Anglo men, local icons. The presentation was always top-down, starting with landowners (male Anglos) who gave land to start and establish the school system. The school system was completely Anglo, including every school board member. Former students were left out entirely. When everything was said and done, there was no mention of the Latino community who labored tirelessly to plant and harvest the crops. I was the only Latino speaker to be invited, and that was organized by former Latina students who were part of my generation. Knowing the situation, I provided an inclusive presentation.

Allow me to amplify some of the traditions, beliefs, and customs of my parents and relatives who came to this country during the tragic decade of the Mexican Revolution. Their folklore was filled with stories of their childhoods, their struggles in coping with the Mexican Revolution, and the transition from northern Mexico to the United States. As in most communities in Mexico, poverty dominated their world, which is one of several reasons why they came to this country. They were not, however, poor in culture. There are long-established traditions brought from their homeland, and these traditions have been reinforced by going back to their original places several times during the years. Food is a classic example of these traditions, in that the food that their children ate was genuinely Mexican in style and flavor, with little influence from the Tex-Mex food found in this country: tamales, chicharrones, *guisados*, corn and flour tortillas, and chorizo Mexicano, among a multitude of products derived from Mexican fine cuisine. The main staple was rice and beans, a long tradition in northern Mexico and, I guess, everywhere else throughout the world. Those two products were on the table all the time. It was basic food and all made by hand at home. There were no trips to restaurants or stores; there were no refrigerators or freezers. All foods were cooked at home, and meat products—hogs, rabbits, doves, and deer, among other animal products—were readily available at the table.

The Catholic religion dominated the entire community. Both communities where my parents were respectively born and raised were surrounded by the Sierra Madre mountains. Besides regular Catholic church attendance, on one of the hills in every community, a *santuario* (sanctuary) was established centuries ago, and since then pilgrimages have been conducted. The purpose of the visitations was many, but mostly it had to do with paying respect for what they got in the name of God or Christ. When we were children, our parents would take us to the foot of the hill and we would walk the long stairs up to the top, where we would kneel down and pray in front of the holy shrine. People came from different locations, including Monterrey, to be part of this pilgrimage at just about any special time of celebration.

At that time the influence of the church on being *compadres* or *comadres* (coparents) was habitual and strong. These religious relations came out of baptizing a child, being *padrino* in a wedding, or just plain wanting to be compadres and comadres. Essentially, the results of these agreement were to gain respect with each other and protect the child by having a second set of parents in case the child needed the protection. These activities created many *ahijados* (godsons) and *ahijadas* (goddaughters). My parents had a lot of compadres and comadres. There was a long tradition of visiting with the compadres on Sundays. The visitations were long and friendly, and the focus was either just to visit or a child that had been baptized. My generation followed these traditions. Personally, I had many compadres. I continue to have affectionate memories of them; we treated ourselves with *cariño* and *amor*. My mother maximized these traditions. For example, when a child was born, a member of the immediate family would baptize the child, meaning that we were compadres. My mother believed that this religious and social arrangements would produce respect, love, and togetherness. Without doubt it worked well! Unfortunately, this relationship is gradually vanishing.

When my parents came from Mexico in the 1910s, the economy of United States, particularly South Texas, was totally agricultural. Economically, farming was traditional and a central base to making a living. During this time that my parents established their roots here, in the 1910s and 1920s, their mode of living was also based on agriculture. With no exception people of Mexican origin worked as sharecroppers. Sharecropping was a legal arrangement in which a landowner allowed sharecroppers to use the land in return for a share of the crops produced on the owner's land. Based on this arrangement the owner would get half of the money produced and the sharecroppers would get the other half, even though they had provided all of the labor and tools. This was a raw deal for the many who had to depend on crops to survive. The patron's expectations were rigid and limitless. There was no major consideration for health, illness, or family matters whatsoever. The focus of the patron was to make gains in his business; sharecroppers' family matters were of no concern of him. Moreover, the amenities provided by the patron were minimal: an old wooden house with dirt floors, no electricity, and no running water. The dwellers that occupied these detestable places were resolved not to ask for much since they could not get it. Although my father made several requests, nothing came of it. There was no tradition of making demands: Mexicans' positions were too fragile and they were sometimes fearful since they could lose their jobs.

Eventually, sharecropping grew to tenant farming. This change allowed a higher economic and social status. By the beginning of the twentieth-first century, about 48 percent of Latinos had acquired middle-class status, according to the US Census.[3] This generation is far more comfortable economically. In legal arrangements to distribute the wealth, Latinos have a better share of this division. Now, we do not have a lot of landowners among Mexican Americans. However, they have small pieces of land, as time goes on they are increasing in land ownership, and they live in better houses with far better amenities, making them more equal than before. In a matter of two generations, life for Mexican Americans is far better in practically every facet.

Another job of the working people was to clear land. From the early twentieth century and on, most land in South Texas was not ready to farm. There was a lot of work in clearing the brush, mesquite, and oak trees for cultivation. This was one of the hardest jobs that new immigrants had to do. The pay to clear acres and acres of land was nominal. During the 1920s my father and Uncle Gregorio worked clearing land during the winter months. They were paid $7.00 for the two to clear one acre of land. The earnings were $3.50 a piece for a whole week. This is enormously hard, especially if you have a family to feed. Clearing land meant that you cut the trees and tree trunks and remove sizeable roots from the ground. Then they had to burn them. This was green wood, which is hard to burn. As the spring arrived, they turned their attention to planting and harvesting, which depended entirely on rain in a semidesert environment.

These changes came with a price. The old customs, traditions, and beliefs have been overturned by mainstream America. Assimilation and acculturation have made the new generation very much like Anglos. The use of the Spanish language is fading and the English language dominates; José, Bonifiacio, Luis, Maria, Blanca, Fernando, and Pasqual are names rarely given to children nowadays. Now we have Eric, Jonathan, Sylvester, Joyce, and Abby, among many other names not found in the history of Mexican Americans. Marriages and weddings have also been changed. The formalities of the past have given way to more practical and less rigid practices; social integration between Anglos and Latinos has come a reality; and intermarriage between Anglos and Hispanics continue to grow. The face of the community has changed forever since intermarriages not only between Latinos and Anglos but also between Latinos and Blacks, Jews, and more. Latinos are now part of a world characterized as intercultural and interracial in practically every matter.

In our community of El Oso we had no contact with professional people, with the exception of medical doctors. We were so far apart socially that it never occurred to anyone to reach for these heights. At least in our minds, we were miles apart. The only contact we had was with Anglo schoolteachers, but, once again, we did not have the characteristics to qualify for these positions. Therefore, in my world, the best thing we could do was take the road less traveled in the hopes that it would get us somewhere and enable us to integrate into the American mainstream. The preservation of our cultural traditions was ultimate. The educational and governmental system was set up for others who had similar values, and, more importantly, this system contained strong elements of repression against minorities.

One hard lesson to learn during my childhood was to overcome the many obstacles such as subordination, segregation, discrimination, and intimidation. On the other hand, we were not overly prepared to fight. These obstacles had been around so long that we accepted them as part of our life. Despite consistent impediments, surrender was never an option. Accepting American culture was not an issue. My family knew that the American system had much to give, and we certainly wanted to be part of the system. However, living close to the US-Mexican border, it is far better to accept the American culture without losing the Mexican culture and its traditions, and I am an example of that.

Like other immigrants to this country, Mexican Americans have made a concerted effort to assimilate and become good citizens. This was against the wishes of many Anglos in our communities. We were not the same as European and Asians immigrants. We have been here for generations way before the United States took the Southwest as the result of the Treaty of Guadalope Hidalgo (1848). There is a significant difference between immigrants from Western Europe and those that come from Mexico and Latin America. The acceptance of color, language, and culture predominated for centuries. Being adjacent to Mexico and Latin America has always been seen as a major threat to people in the United States. The language is different, most of them are mestizos (darker color of skin), and they have a different culture and traditions. It was true more than a hundred years ago just like it is today. Regardless of these realities, we had no choice but to integrate and defend the integrity of who we were. Although our goal was to coexist and integrate, the governmental policies of the state of Texas were focused on the eradication of our language and culture, as I experienced in the school system.

I was never unhappy or antisocial. I had traumatic experiences, but I managed to take them in stride and was always hopeful that there was a better future around the corner. In normal circumstances I sought mechanisms for change to bridge the two dominant cultures—Latinos and Anglos. The gap between the two was so wide that I followed the concept of "fake it until you make it." I was a conformist in the school environment as a way to be accepted, but conformity only lasted until I matured and became myself, a different person. In the school system, I was never myself. I felt that if I were, I wouldn't last in that environment. When I was young I was quiet and practically never spoke at school, yet I was outspoken at home. I was a joiner, and I always put on a smile when facing the social and cultural barriers at school. It certainly was a way to protect myself and survive, and it had its dividends. Since early childhood I was never confrontational or expressive on these critical issues. I was subtle, mental, and patient. All these characteristics require compromise. I much prefer to compromise with myself before I compromise with others. In other words, you do not want to be taken in by others that are more powerful than you are. This has been my model to promote cultural coexistence and to create a stronger overlapping society.

During my early years, it was rare for a person of Mexican origin to own a house or land. This has changed, and although we have a way to go, we continue to gain and break ground in many areas. Politically, our clout has increased somewhat, our voices are rising, and the fears of the traditional established group have grown. But there are many contradictions. The road continues to be rocky, and we have a long way to go before we reach parity. The forces against the growth of minorities are still in existence, but the silent voices of the past are not very silent anymore. One must evaluate the current role that Latinos have played to realize how much has changed and how most of the change has been for the better.

We have been truly fortunate to have lived through all the ups and downs of a difficult and challenging life connected with three generations. I hope that I will do some justice to the work and the many folks who have been neglected and never given credit for their contributions. The exploitation of Mexican labor in the twentieth century is well documented. My parents, like others, were part of this dreadful exploitation. According to John Weber in *From South Texas to the Nation: The Exploitation of Mexican Labor in the Twentieth Century*, in a matter of a decade, the region of South Texas, which was often considered too isolated for farming, "became one of the United States' most lucrative farming regions and one of its worst places to work."[4] In the early 1940s and 1950s, I caught the tail end of this incredible labor exploitation.

It never occurred to me when I was growing up that the world we were living in would change as much as it has. In rural and farming areas of South Texas we lived a very quiet life in a world characterized by economic entrenchment as laborers without much voice or say in the affairs of our economic, political, and social life. We lived at the bottom of a class-structured society as migrants that reflected the history of Mexico and spilled into the southern United States. In chapter 2 I will offer different accounts of family life in rural South Texas during the 1940s and 1950s.

Chapter 2

Family Life in Rural South Texas

Rural living in South Texas was tough and rigorous. Life was crowned by major doses of hard labor and limited resources. Economically, it was truly an unending adventure of ups and downs, with little if any economic stability under a well-established patron system. Socially, we were marginalized, originally by Mexicans from Mexico and then by Anglos. Politically, we were apolitical with no detectable influence. I had a nonparticipatory family, completely disenfranchised. Educationally, like the rest of the Mexican American community, we considered ourselves *muy jodidos* (all beaten up), as my Godfather Rumaldo used to say. Yet despite these hardships, we lived a normal and satisfying life.

My mother was the center of the house, assisted by my Aunt Lupita and other members of the family. She ran a tight ship. Mama handled the work with diplomacy, discretion, respect, and firmness. Her conduct was so sophisticated that she appeared not to lift a finger in the decision-making process. She truly masterminded home relations since she was fully in charge of the internal activities at home. Dad would not interfere with home affairs. His job was to work externally with family and others, give us discipline and good skills, and bring the bread home. Later, when some of my siblings got married, my mother would welcome the in-laws with love, charm, and respect. I can say with pride that every one of us loved her to the utmost, including every in-law. She was loved, respected, and at times feared.

For the size of our extended family, the house was very small. The dilapidated conditions of our home made it difficult to accommodate everyone. There was neither electricity nor running water. We had to haul the water from a nearby *papalote* (windmill). Only a small part of the house had wooden floors; the rest were dirt floors, including the kitchen, where my mother cooked three square meals a day, seven days a week, for twelve to fifteen people. Despite these limitations my mother kept the place spotless.

The wooden frame of the house was flimsy, comprised of one-inch-thick pieces of wood boards with no insulation. We did not even know that insulation existed. The metal roof was just above our heads, and the windows were made from wood. When it rained, we could hear every drop that fell on the roof. Sometimes it was comforting to hear the raindrops since it meant no work on the fields the next day. The rain also promised a good crop to harvest since we lived in a semiarid area of Texas. There was little room for beds, so all of us slept on the floor. It is amazing how when you do not have beds you can accommodate a lot of people in one room. There were no bathrooms and only one outhouse, and the lack of electricity created a natural darkness inside and a sound of deep silence unknown in today's world. Despite these conditions, somehow it did not bother us. We knew that most of the Anglos had bathroom facilities inside their homes; all we needed to do to wait into we could afford it. Finally, it came in the fall of 1962, which was also the first year I taught school, and it was in Pawnee. As soon as I got my first monthly check, I discussed the matter with my parents. Bathroom facilities were installed for the first time ever.

To accommodate all of us, we had an additional home nearby where *tias* (aunts) Lupita and Nina, my father's sisters, and some of us lived. Lupita, the oldest of the *tias*, was a fireball. We all loved and respected her. She was a force to contend with. Like Dad, she was *repelona* (cranky). Yet she loved her family, and she tirelessly worked for the betterment of the entire family. It wasn't until I was a teenager that I was able to have a small bed that I shared with my cousin Remijio, who died in his 30s in a truck accident while hauling dirt. We had a storm cellar that my dad built because my mother was terrified of windstorms and lightning. This served well during major storms. Every time we were threatened with bad weather, all of us would run to the cellar. The storm cellar was built by digging a spot six by twelve feet and deep enough so we could stand up inside. Once it was dug, railroad logs were laid, followed by pieces of wood, then it was covered by dirt. The stairs were also made of dirt. We felt very safe when we had to be there.

We had no running water, so we had to haul it from a windmill about a quarter of a mile away. To carry the water from the windmill to the house, my father built a *rastra* (sled) made out of two mesquite logs with wooden logs across these, and it was pulled by two mules. Two water barrels (110 gallons) would provide water for all of us and for everything except for washing our clothes. My mother, my four sisters, and I would go to the *papalote* once a week. It was a whole-day affair. We would bring our *talladores* (wash boards to scrub), which were handmade by a neighbor from Mexico. The *talladores* were made in different sizes depending on the size of the individual. Mine was the smallest since I was the *coyote* of the clan.

Part of our livelihood was to move north as soon as we finished harvesting the crops in South Texas. By early September Dad would start making plans to migrate north in search of work. Cars were rare in El Oso at that time. We had one old truck for dozens of people to travel. Dad would do most of the driving. He would visit with neighbors to see if their families would migrate with us. Most of the work was picking cotton. Normally, four or five families would join us for a three-to-four-month journey. For this annual journey, the truck became home for thirty to forty people while we looked for temporary housing. We waited until we celebrated Diez y Seis de

Septiembre (September 16), Mexico's Independence Day. This celebration was capped by a celebration at a dance hall either in Karnes City (Salon Benito Juarez) or in Kenedy (Salon Monterrey). This involved a series of ceremonies following patriotic and historical Mexican traditions, including the coronation of a queen. For those living in a Mexican enclave, this was one of the biggest celebrations of the year. Obviously, my generation knew that we were Americans, but we were living with our parents and grandparents' traditions. Any major level of assimilation into the American way of life was still years away.

The first major stop on the journey was San Antonio, seventy miles away. Led by my mother, it was our tradition to visit El Señor de los Milagros, a private chapel on the Westside of San Antonio. There, my mother and the rest of the group would pray, contribute money, and light a candle or two for a safe journey and a safe return. Upon our return from *las piscas* (picking cotton), we would visit the chapel to pay our respects. This was a yearly affair for all the trips that we made north of where we were born and raised.

I always wanted to go to school, even if it was for a week or two, and my parents gave their approval. At times I would attend school for two to three weeks. At that time parts of Northwest Texas had few residents of Mexican origin. There, the level of discrimination was far lower, and we were well accepted. The students and teachers at these rural schools were fascinated by our cultural background. Although there was not much learning, it really felt good to be welcomed.

It was understood that for us to survive, both in South Texas and on the path we traveled north, we had to support each other. Although this provided a mechanism for protection and survival, it prevented us from assimilating, acculturating, and integrating into mainstream America. What were these factors that prevented us from assimilating? For example: As a group we were inseparable, not allowing Anglos to penetrate our world; not knowing the English language was a significant barrier; we had a level of subordination that kept us on the sidelines; and our cultural differences created a natural separation from other people that were different than us. There was no plan to assimilate and integrate; it just happened over time. But integration in South Texas was difficult because we were subordinated as inferiors. The situation was even more complicated because when we visited our family in Mexico, we were considered foreigners (Tejanos), so we were neither from here nor from there. We needed to make a transition to another culture, but somehow we were not ready to commit ourselves. Moreover, we were too close to Mexico. As we know most immigrants came from Europe and Asia, and survival meant to assimilate and acculturate rapidly. In our situation, it was not easy to assimilate since discrimination was rampant in South Texas.

When we were at home in South Texas, the home cooking was great—all Mexican food. My mother and aunts did a masterful job. Migrating north of South Texas radically changed our eating habits, whether we liked it or not. Our Mexican food staples were not found in the grocery stores, including canned food. Once we situated ourselves more permanently along the way, my mother did everything possible to prepare food that was more to our liking.

Migrating every year of my childhood was truly an adventure. The adventure was far more challenging for my parents, who had the responsibility not only of their family but also of several families that accompanied us. The cultural difference was significant as to how these folks treated people of Mexican origin. As time went on, however, the cultural climate changed since the population growth of Mexican Americans became considerable. There is a simple correlation to these cultural differences. The more Mexican Americans migrated there, the greater the social prejudices. Our experiences there came when very few Mexican Americans migrated. Prejudice and social anxiety were not present, but as time went on, the population grew, things changed, and it began to have the peculiarity of South Texas. The economic climate of the region was far better and more advanced than South Texas. Cotton and groundwater irrigation made life easier for the owners and for us that supplied the labor force. There the normal number of pounds of cotton that we picked was three times more per day than South Texas, and the pay was higher. The owners gave more humane treatment to the workers. Simply put, the economic environment in Northwest Texas was far better than South Texas.

The socioeconomic climate among the cotton pickers was less competitive since this area was wealthier than South Texas. The only social place that we met with other migrants was on Saturday, when we would go shopping to buy groceries and other vital items. Our relations were pleasant as we exchanged how we saw the place and the work that we were doing. On Saturday the business owners would receive us with open arms. There was another group that were contracted to come to the United States to work. They were Mexicans from southern Mexico. With no social hostility that we could experience, our cultural differences set us apart. We were so physically and socially apart that the only communication was when we would come on Saturday, and even there it was limited. For the cotton owners, it was a private matter among them, migrants, and government.

As a migrant, temporarily attending school in Northwest Texas was socially and culturally far more favorable than attending Cadillac Elementary back home. After many years of navigating from place to place to find work, we finally settled on a farm north of Lockney, Texas. Lone Star Elementary became our center of education away from home. Compared with Cadillac, Lone Star Elementary was enormously different. For the first time in my formal schooling, I became myself, just the way I was at home. I had far more social freedom, and I was accepted and integrated with ease. I became a cultural icon since Anglos in the community had a fascination with Mexican culture.

Social life in our community was severely limited. Tradition, space, and time were important factors that contributed to these limitations. In the El Oso community, there was not a single place that one could assemble to socialize or discuss issues affecting the community. The El Oso store was one of two places where we came together; the food store and the cotton gin were owned by a group of German Americans. During the summer cotton pickers would bring wagons with cotton to be ginned. The cotton pickers were all Mexicans, because no Anglo farmers would pick cotton. With all the work involved, while they waited for the cotton to be ginned, they would visit and exchange ideas and promote conversations. When the opportunity was present, I would try to come along with Dad in the hope that I would see *mi padrino* (godfather), Hilario Chapa, who baptized me. If he was there, he would give me a nickel for a soda or a piece of candy. It was great because sodas and candy were not found at home, and money was hard to come by. Socially, many of the visits we made were done while we worked the fields. Although the work was hard, and it was done in the middle of the summer when temperatures were consistently around 100 degrees, in addition to the persistent humidity of South Texas, it gave us the opportunity to connect with other neighbors. I have great memories of those days.

Any social gathering would be at the church, which was miles away in Pawnee, and automobiles were not available for the trip. The church in Pawnee did not have a hall for any kind of association, and the priest would come from Three Rivers (a community fifteen miles away) for Sunday mass, after which he would immediately return. This is still true today. The other alternative for socializing was a place for dancing in the small community of Nell, Texas, where the organizer of the event was Polo Zamora. Polo built a *plataforma* (a dance floor made out of cement, out in the open) behind a store that had a cantina, all owned by an Anglo by the last name of Franke. The Friday night dances were very popular with the Mexican American folks in the community. Conjunto music was at its peak during the 1950s and 1960s, and musicians were contracted to come and play. This weekly affair during the summer months went beyond dancing. People played bingo, and fast food was available.

We attended church occasionally when we had wheels and/or the weather was good, since we had dreadful dirt roads. The small church (Our Lady of Guadalupe Catholic Church) located in Pawnee facilitated services for the entire Catholic community. It was not until years later that a small hall for social gatherings emerged, and it is still operating today. Moreover, during the summer months, it was common to go to Kenedy to buy clothes and groceries and to socialize. Instead of socializing at the plaza as we did in Mexico, we socialized on the streets of Kenedy. These Saturday excursions provided the opportunity to catch up with the community *chisme* (gossip) and, perhaps, to meet girlfriends or boyfriends, or even future husbands or wives. Many of these social activities were done openly in the streets or at the pharmacy, where ice cream and sodas were found. We always looked forward to the next Saturday to continue our visits. Going to the movie theater was rare. By the time I got to high school, an Anglo theater in Kenedy had become integrated, so we were able to see American movies for the first time, while television was still in its infancy.

These were the formal social aspects of the community of El Oso. This was just the beginning. Humans find ways to socialize regardless of social conditions. Informally, space and time were an open-ended affair. We learned to socialize with our folks and others at every opportunity that presented itself. It was fun and joyful. Practically every Sunday afternoon, my parents and family would visit or were visited by nearby friends. These Sunday visits were all-day affairs. Being friends and being *compadres* and *comadres* (coparents) were common. *Compadrismo* and *comadrisma* (a social relationship between being parents and being godparents) were common in our cultural surroundings. This social marriage between families has faded considerably over time. The idea of the whole family coming together on Sundays is a thing of the past.

Since technology was limited, most work was done manually. The opportunity to come together to work was natural for relatives, neighbors, and other people that would come to work with us. There was humor and entertainment, including *corridos* (ballads) like the "Corrido del Paso," played by my Uncle Gregorio. It never occurred to me that I would live in this beautiful city.

When I was a child, my dad would take us to see Mexican movies. Although there was a theater in Kenedy (the nearest town to us), only Anglos were allowed to participate. Since we were not able to see movies in Anglo theaters, we would go to *carpas* (tents) to see old Mexican movies. It was a joy to see old movies since we knew something about the Mexican actors. The center of news and entertainment was the Spanish radio station (KCOR) and *La Prensa*, a weekly Spanish newspaper published in San Antonio. There were three main elements that helped us to learn to read and write in Spanish. First, my parents were insistent that we learn how to read and write our native language. Second, my parents sent me to visit Abundio Chapa, a friend and neighbor, to expand my ability to read and write. Don Abundio was an older man who was completely blind, but he was the most educated person in the community. He was a Mexican who came to the United States as an adult. He had a few books about history and geography, and he would ask me to read them out loud as he listened intently. Invariably, he would correct my pronunciation and define words I was unfamiliar with. I would write sentences and read them to him for corrections and interpretations. The narrative of my thoughts and reading assignments were all in Spanish and all done with our own folks.

Other than business or school, there was virtually no contact with the Anglo community. When we visited Anglo homes, it was strictly for business, which was conducted outside on the steps of the house. The same was true when Anglos came to our homes for business. As far as I know, the first Anglo who entered our house did so in 1963 when I had the mumps, and I was already teaching in Pawnee. The junior high principal who came to visit was not from the local area. We were operating in isolation. The road to assimilation and acculturation was narrow, and we often paid no attention.

Our food supply came from San Antonio. Dad and mom would visit a group of Chinese merchants located where El Mercado is now, just south of the Plaza de Zacate (Milan Park) and across from Santa Rosa Hospital. During the 1940s and 1950s, this area was considered the Westside of San Antonio, where most Mexicans lived. During World War II, commodities of all kinds were hard to obtain, including basic staples such as beans, potatoes, rice, and flour. Still, Dad managed to get enough staples for our big family. Since I was the youngest of the family, I normally accompanied my parents. I often lobbied for things that I wanted. I would target my mother for items I thought she was able to obtain. I knew that if I could convince her, she would take care of the rest. Since our parents had limited resources, most of my efforts were fruitless. Yet there was always food on the table. I cannot express enough my appreciation for my parents' love and care and for their great struggle to keep us fed and protected in a world difficult to survive. The struggles and hardships that my parents endured to give us and members of our community a better life was incomparable. Their compassion and generosity to people in need goes beyond comprehension.

The economy in the 1940s to the 1960s in rural South Texas was sustained by labor-intensive agricultural farming. The farms were owned by Anglos, and within those farms there were clusters of Mexican families working for the patron, Nick Lynch. For the most part, Mexican Americans were sharecroppers, powerless and dependent on an unfair economic system. This is where I was born and raised by an immigrant family composed of parents, aunts, uncles, and other relatives; some were not related but needed a place to work, eat, and rest. For me this was the center of the universe; this is where I played with my double cousins and where we gathered and had family reunions. It was an unconditionally safe place where family life reigned and the spirit of work was pronounced. Life on the farm was mostly serene since we stayed in one place, only going to town once a week and, if we were lucky, to the Friday night dances during the summer months. Our surroundings were isolated, always tinted by hard work, and the culture was exclusively Mexican.

At the farm it was more than eight-to-five working conditions. Breakfast would start at six, and we would immediately proceed to go to the field to plow, plant, and grow or pick cotton, corn, broomcorn, and sorghum. In this semiarid area, there were often droughts that placed major hardships on families. We would work the entire day with an hour's break for lunch and then come home at dusk. Under ordinary circumstances we would work long days for five to six days a week. During times of harvest, particularly when it threatened to rain, we would practically work around the clock. This was the way we survived, and there was no way to change it. My father, a hard-driven and fearless man, set the tone for our work ethic, and he was the boss. He expected quality and quantity of himself and those around him, and he got it.

My parents were children of the Mexican Revolution, which prompted a wave of immigrants to the United States to escape the violence across the Rio Bravo. My father came to this country when he was 12, and my mother came when she was 13. Like many immigrants their hopes were to return home one day, but like most that never happened. Both my parents crossed the river legally since there were no immigration laws at the time. My father came from Villaldama and my mother from Sabinas Hidalgo, Nuevo León. These small communities were located between Monterrey and Nuevo Laredo.

After six hard years of labor in Laredo and in search of a better life, my father moved north. Even in his teens my father was responsible for feeding his mother and three sisters. Dad lost his father when he was 7 years old, and by tradition he automatically became the head of the family at this young age. He managed to make a connection with a landowner in Bee County in the small community of Monteola. In 1918 my father, accompanied by my Uncle Pancho, followed the railroad tracks to San Antonio via Kenedy. It was a difficult journey since neither man had any money or knew anybody. Every time my wife Norma and I drive through Fall City on our way to the farm where I grew up, we think of the story that Dad told us about arriving in this community by following the railroad tracks. They were tired and hungry and literally begging for food and water. A couple of Mexican immigrants, a wife and husband, came to the rescue. They fed them and packed them some lunch for the remainder of their journey. My mother followed suit, to Monteola to join family members. My father and mother met in Laredo before they came to this community. They soon got engaged, and their courtship lasted for five years. In 1923 they were married by a Catholic priest in a barn near where I was born and raised in El Oso.

As a child I saw my mother as a tireless individual who started her day around four thirty in the morning. She would turn the radio on and listen to music from radio stations as far away as Mexico City. She loved music, and she learned to play the guitar. She was warm and friendly, diplomatic to the core. She was also calculating, tenacious, cool, and determined to do whatever was possible for the family. She directed the traffic for the entire family, including my father. She was so good at it that it was unnoticeable. She had an extraordinary talent for mediating and balancing family struggles. For Mom, home was her *reinado* (kingdom), and she ran it with a firm hand but also with love, passion, compassion, great precision, quietness, grace, and a belt near her for her youngest son. I feared the belt because she put it to good use when I behaved badly. Being in a large household, she was always surrounded by other women to assist her since the men never meddled with the kitchen or any part of the interior of the house. She needed this help since she had to produce an average of fifteen full meals three times a day. She managed to do it seven days a week, which is just incredible. The circumstances under which my mother and other women had to operate were acts of bravery.

As a child living with a large family, it would have been easy for me to be lost in the crowd. I thought that I was the brightest of the bunch, but that was far from the truth. I was just one of the kids, and I am glad. My parents treated the family in the best way they could to be fair, just, and equal. Yet like in other families, my sisters took a back seat to the boys in terms of freedom and access. Fortunately, this is not true anymore. In this generation more than ever, the women in my family have taken a role equal to men, and they are teaching their kids to do the same. Machismo does not exist in my family anymore.

My mother had a strong sense of belonging; she kept track of all of us, and she knew far more than any one of us ever imagined. She was shrewd and skilled in delegating authority. She was a disciplinarian, and I had a share of that discipline from time to time. My curiosity and intuition sometimes got the best of me, and I would get in trouble. This curiosity gave me the ability to be manipulative with my sisters, but that was not enough for Mom. My sister Minerva consistently catered to the multiple silly ideas and grandeurs that I had and still have. In her efforts to defend me, she would end up in serious trouble too. As a good child, many of my doings were nothing earthshaking. It was intuition and curiosity to pry into a world unknown to me.

I spent most of my life exploring, though I did not know why. These explorations went without much interference from my family. I was not lonely by any means. I remained quiet and isolated from the family as I tried to figure out an unknown path. My life has been filled with optimism. Somehow, I felt that if I kept thinking about it, my eyes would open to new horizons. On these matters I rarely if ever shared my feelings with my brothers and sisters. I had a desire to gradually transform to another world that I knew little about.

The Escamilla family (Ofelia, Gollo, Chindo, Edelmiro, Beto, Gloria, Uncle Gregorio, and Aunt Chita) lived near us, and we would see each other daily. In early fall of every year, we migrated northwest with them and other families. We were inseparable, and for the most part our relations were good. We were double cousins of the siblings of the Escamillas.

The oldest of the Escamilla siblings was Ofelia. When she was born, my parents were asked to baptize her, becoming the *padrino* and *madrina* (godfather and godmother) of Ofelia. From then on every member of the family started calling my parents godmother and godfather. Throughout my childhood the Escamillas' children called me *Beto* (short for Roberto) *el de madrina* since one of my double cousins was also known as Beto (short for Alberto). Although throughout our childhood we were inseparable, three major events gave us different roads to travel, and our relationship changed, at least for me. By the time we finished junior high school, Chindo decided that he would not attend school any longer. He was the last remaining relative who dropped out of school. From there on as far as family, school was a solo act. It was unusual since we had been together since birth.

Theother change occurred when I left for university. While I was in high school, we continued to visit and socialize, including organizing a *conjunto* to play regional music in different parts of the community. Finally, Gollo (Gregorio) and Chindo (Reducindo) married far sooner than I did, and their families really turned in different directions. It was never the same, and, unfortunately and unnecessarily, our social distances widened as time went on to the point of not talking to or visiting each other (Gollo in this case) for years. When I saw Gollo again, it was at his funeral. It is a true and sad commentary: *pero asi es la vida* (such is life).

Gradually and unwillingly, I departed from my cultural roots as I pursued higher education. Even when I started my educational career, I did not have high hopes that I would finish. When I started university, I was hoping that I would last for at least six weeks. My thought processes told me that as soon as my professors knew my capability, I would be out of there. I had a lot of ambition, but my lack of self-confidence told me that after six weeks at the university I would be told that it was time for me to go back home since I was unable to pass the courses. Regardless of the consequences, I had a story tell my relatives and friends—namely, that I had gone to the university. In the meantime, the Army was waiting for me anyway. It never occurred to me that I would remain at the university for the rest of my professional career.

Here is a statement from an unknown source that defines how I was thinking and doing in my early years: "REST IN PEACE to the opportunities we missed because of shyness and low self-esteem."

The cultural gap between schools and Latino families was enormously wide. It wasn't until the second or third generation that school attendance and success became more of a reality. Yet despite the lack of educational opportunities, most of my family members have done well in their lives. Unquestionably, my parents raised a talented group of children with the abilities and courage to take on the world, as well as anyone else. This was done in an environment of limited economic opportunities; under the brunt of racial, ethnic, and social discrimination; and facing a lack of the formal education bestowed on other, more fortunate groups.

In my parents' generation as well as my generation, Tejanos fought back and pursued middle-class status; there was considerable resistance against oppressors, not only to preserve our culture but also to learn the "American way." It has been a hard road, but our efforts as a family made a considerable difference to the next generation, who faced a different set of issues. The consequences of this struggle were numerous. Yet we fought ethnic and class differences, racial profiling, discrimination, and lack of justice and equality. The laws of our local, state, and national governments exceedingly sided with those who made the laws. Although conditions have changed, the government continues to side with those that are wealthy and more powerful, regardless of race, ethnicity, or gender.

The first and second generation of Latinos in higher education have not experienced anything close to what past generations did. Access to the school system has changed. Now, a considerable number of Tejanas and Tejanos have become middle-class, and parents are far more active in school affairs. Now, when major tragedies have occurred, voices from Latinos have risen, they fight courageously and expect answers to their questions and concerns. This monumental accomplishment of political and social activity would have never happened a generation or two ago. Another illustration of middle-class activity can be found in my large family, which typifies other families. We come together to celebrate in a rural setting, and we celebrate a lot. All the members of the family are middle-class, and this membership is ethnically diversified by marriages. Anglos are part of us, and we are part of them. I am the last male member of my family from my generation. It is hard to believe that the runt of the family is now considered the "patriarch." How times change!

Today, the community continues to be rural, but unlike yesteryear it is not an agricultural community. It is based on cattle ranching and oil. Although most of the land is still possessed by Anglos, the landscape began to change in my generation, with most Anglos moving to urban areas for better jobs and a different life. A good number of

Hispanics have remained in rural areas simply because their families have enough strength to remain together and there were no jobs of any significance in town. Pawnee, where I went to high school, was once an Anglo community and is now Hispanic.

During my first year of teaching at Bee County College in Beeville, I got a telephone call from a family member of George Hines. I was told that George, who was one of my classmates in high school, had died in a traffic accident. I was asked if I could be one of the pallbearers, and I accepted the invitation. At the funeral at the Baptist Church in Pawnee, there was not a single Mexican American. I am convinced that I was the first Latino to ever step foot in that church. From there George was taken to the Pawnee Cemetery. Once again, I was the first person of Mexican origin to step within the cemetery grounds. The Mexican American cemetery is a quarter mile away on the other side of the road. This is where many of my relatives are buried. In this cemetery, only one Anglo, my brother-in-law who was married to my sister Minerva, has been buried. Today, the Baptist Church is occupied mainly by Latinos since the number of Anglos living there is very small and many Mexican American are not Catholic anymore. The cemeteries continue to be segregated, at least in this area.

Changes are occurring at all levels in South Texas. Latino high school graduates and college graduates are growing in numbers. Moreover, land and home owning has increased immensely in this population, as has renting land to raise cattle. Nick Lynch owned thousands of acres where dozens of Mexican American families worked for years; it is now run by a nephew of mine to raise cattle. There are no workers out in the field anymore since most jobs are in town or elsewhere, and these folks drive to work daily and come home at the end of the day. As a result of these many changes, Tejanos and Anglos are coming together. More than ever, they depend on each other. Nonetheless, Latinos have less wealth than Anglos, and the public schools are still run mainly by Anglos.

For the many of us who came from the lower socioeconomic ranks, leading in the field of higher education is something short of a miracle.

We sought a new world that would provide us with dignity, respect, and a voice to speak on behalf of our community. These fundamental human rights were denied to our forefathers in South Texas and elsewhere. Moreover, we seek a strong voice for understanding and recognizing our cultural heritage and language because we have been ready to share it. Despite all these struggles, it has been a powerful experience full of excitement and rewards. We are passing the baton to future generations. If I have concerns, it is that I want the new generation to understand that nothing worthwhile comes easily, and there is still more to do.

Latino contributions to the community and nation are rarely recognized. For example, one time the owner of the El Oso cotton gin came to visit me. I was alone at home since my family had migrated north following the fall crops. This was the first time in my life that I had stayed behind so I could attend school full-time. Amanda Weston, the owner of the cotton gin, asked if I could give her a hand in loading an eighteen-wheeler truck of cotton seed to be shipped elsewhere. I accepted and joined the workers who were ready to start loading the truck. We worked for almost twelve hours. I came home exhausted to make dinner. I did not know if she was going to pay me or not. Two weeks later, I saw Amanda, and she told me that she owed me $3.00. However, instead of giving me the $3.00, she gave me a forty-pound bag of cotton seed. She knew that I was raising a steer for the upcoming spring stock show. This kind of economic relationship between owners and laborers was common. Today, undocumented workers receive similar treatment in South Texas and elsewhere.

In chapter 3 I compare and contrast the social, economic, and political relations between Latinos and Anglos over time. Social distance was considerable in my generation. Politically, there was no match; we were apolitical. Economically, we engaged in owner-laborer relations. As I will discuss in the epilogue, in the last two generations, a lot of these issues have gradually changed, and they have changed for the better. In terms of equity with Anglos, we have a ways to go. For example, ownership of land is practically all possessed by Anglos in South Texas.

Chapter 3

Mexican Americans and Anglos in Rural South Texas

The El Oso community provided a rich background for families of Mexican origin and Anglos to come together. In my early years, the Tejano family had a strong family tradition. At the time it was very Catholic, and for the most part, the Latino community had a high sense of optimism. In spite of the social and economic conditions, the Mexican American community was determined to take the blows and move on. Yet these folks had humility, innocence, and sometimes a lack of desire to fight for their causes. Growing up in a large and extended family, we accepted our socioeconomic status with grace and determination, with the sincere hope that life was going to become better. Ultimately, it did. The Anglo community was quieter and more subtle. Although encounters with Tejanos were part of their daily lives, for the most part there was no hostility. Secretly and quietly both groups had some admiration and compassion with each other. As we know, love and care by humans have no boundaries. Yet both Anglos and Latinos kept boundaries to protect themselves and to make sure that they were different. This relationship was not symmetrical. Because of differences in power relations, Latinos consistently gave in more to

Anglos. This was not a question of desire to give in to Anglos; it was a tradition and necessity. In other words, Anglos were "insiders," and Mexican Americans were "outsiders."

Beyond the ethnic and cultural factors, there was a social factor that separated the two groups. Generally, Mexican Americans viewed the Anglos with admiration, respect, and honor. Some preferred Anglos over our own folks. In this relationship the Anglos looked down on us, and they were not the only ones. Middle-class Mexicans saw us as lesser and often showed a lack of respect. Mexicans from Mexico had considerable trouble understanding our plight as exercised by the whites. When we compared how Mexicans and Anglos viewed us, social distance and isolation were far worse with our Anglo counterparts. For example, when I started college, Anglo classmates would ride to the university with me back every week, but we never socialized, nor was I invited to their homes.

The political culture of South Texas is filled with ironies driven by the sweeping winds of multiple groups, including Native Americans, Spaniards, Mexicans, and Anglos. The Rio Grande River, which separates the United States from Mexico, has been the center of two overlapping European cultures coexisting with Native Americans. The Southern Hemisphere was occupied by Spain, France, and the Mediterranean, while the Northern Hemisphere was occupied by England and Scandinavian countries. Neil Foley in his book *The White Scourge: Mexicans, Blacks, and Poor Whites in Texas Cotton Culture* claims that "it was a site of multiple and heterogeneous borders where different languages, experiences, histories, and voices intermingled amid diverse relations of power and privilege."[1]

In the last two generations, there have been major population shifts. The era of Mexican migration started during the Mexican Revolution and continued through the 1930s, 1940s, and 1950s, significantly increasing the Mexican population in South Texas. Further population shifts occurred starting in the 1950s as migration from rural areas to urban areas populated large cities like San Antonio, Houston, Corpus Christi, and many other destinations in Texas and elsewhere.

By the 1980s a large percentage of the Mexican American population was located in urban centers. These population shifts contributed to the reduction of Anglos in rural areas. Anglo political dominance continued to dissipate. Most Anglos (like Blacks earlier) left their farms and ranches in South Texas for urban areas. During this time the Latino population increased considerably, even in rural areas. The twentieth-century migration of rural people to cities changed the landscape and the political and economic dynamics of South Texas. Richard Parker's book *Lone Star Nation: How Texas Will Transform America* summarizes this transformation: "By the end of 2013, one thing was abundantly clear: The era of Anglo dominance in Texas was all but over."[2] Although Parker's statement has some validity, we are still suffering from Anglo dominance in Texas and South Texas.

There were strong elements in the Anglo social structure that revealed their lack of desire to understand our culture. This holds true for immigrants as well, particularly if they are not from Western Europe. What we had to offer did not count. We do not, however, compromise our values to satisfy the Anglo community. The strength of our culture, family, religion, hard work, love for our country; the honored place of our mothers and fathers; and protecting our way of life for children have remained strong. Naturally, we did not like our status, but at that time choices were extremely limited.

Let me provide two daunting examples of this phenomenon. First, Dad, like many Mexican immigrants, work enormously hard to make a living. It was all manual work done by using an axe and a pick. During his early life, his job was to clear acres of land so farming could be done. Dad and Uncle Gregorio would clear an acre a week. This involved cutting trees and everything down and burning it to the ground to be ready for farming. Both men would earn a total of seven dollars a week to clear an acre of land. Anyone who can do this kind of difficult work should be recognized; their work should be valued. After all, without clearing the land, there will be no farming.

The second example has to do with building the Hemisfair and the Tower of the Americas in San Antonio in the late 1960s. In a written document done by the "builders" on recognizing and giving credit for doing this remarkable work, practically nothing was mentioned of the bricklayers or cement workers or Mexicans. Credits went to Texans in high positions, the leadership of the San Antonio community, Spain, and a few others.[3] That being said, labor was not valued and those doing the labor were people of Mexican origin. The subtitle of John Weber's book *From South Texas to the Nation* makes it very explicit: *The Exploitation of Mexican Labor in the Twentieth Century*.

Like many others, my childhood was a compelling story of failures and successes, sometimes under the most trying circumstances. It is a narrative of struggles, poverty, survival, and the clash of cultural values. But it is also a story of love, fear, humility, apprehension, pride, and a strong longing to do good and break through social, ethnic, and class barriers. We were trampled in the name of assimilation and acculturation and denied integration into the social and educational system. Yet we conquered our limitations and difficulties under these difficult circumstances. We must reach parity with other groups. This will help to have a better understanding and offer higher levels of cooperation among each other. In a novel by Arturo Islas, *The Rain Gods*, the author tells of how Chico (the fictional name for himself), coming from humble beginnings, struggles through school life and was able to become a university professor. Now, at that time, thinking of being a university professor was totally out of mind, completely out of the picture for me.

Once I was invited to be the keynote speaker at a state association of community colleges in Colorado. The topic was immigration. After a lengthy presentation, it was time for questions and answers. The organizer and person who introduced me asked a pointed question: "Sir, could you tell us how you managed to get here, or how you managed to be here standing before us?" Understanding the depth of her question, I provided a simple answer: "I took Interstate 25 from El Paso to Denver, then I took Interstate 40, and this is how we arrived here!" She smiled and she said, "No, no, no, I read your curriculum vitae and wondered how you managed to get to be a university professor?" I asked myself, How do you answer that? My wife was in the audience, and she raised her hand and asked if she could comment. Naturally, I agreed. She said, "He is very stubborn, I know!" We had a good laugh, and we moved on. Coming home to El Paso I kept thinking about her question and its derivatives. This was my conclusion: When I was asked to speak, I sent a thirty-six-page curriculum vitae. The résumé had a wide range of activities from being named as "one of one hundred most influentials Hispanics in the United States" by *Hispanic Business* magazine to being a Fulbright Scholar in Mexico.

The world of my childhood consisted of two families: Villarreal (my father) and Escamilla (my mother). The Villarreal family was huge and economically poor, with Spanish, Native American, and Jewish origins. My father, Epifanio, was not overly diplomatic, spoke matter of factly, and was not as sociable as my mother. On the other hand, he was honest, straightforward, very intelligent, and the most hardworking person I have ever known. But he would speak out with considerable force. *El hombre no tenia pelos en la lengua!* (The man did not have hair on his tongue!) He did not tolerate nonsense, and he would let you know it, straight and explicit.

The Escamilla family was different. They lived on the lighter side of life and enjoyed it. In many ways they were the life of the party. They loved music; they enjoyed singing and playing instruments, and many of their physical traits had a level of biological dominance seen today in several members of the family, including me. My mother loved music, loved to sing and play the guitar. Never to be underestimated, my mother was bright, tough, and diplomatic to the core. The Escamilla family was a joyful group, though vulnerable and somewhat fearful. They were lovers, and I have the distinction of being part of that, and my wife knows that well. Dad had a lot of influence in both families. He was feared by many. Once, we got in trouble for seeking various avenues to hear music. We had a distant neighbor who was a Christian fundamentalist. Part of their religious ceremonies was praying and singing. Knowing this, my cousins Gregorio, Chindo, and

I decided to attend a nightly gathering without permission from my parents. We had a good understanding between the three of us that no word would be said about what we planned to do, so we went. Well, guess what? When we arrived, the whole group was singing loud and clear, and Uncle Daniel Escamilla was in the middle of the bunch with a guitar in hand, singing his life away. Our family was all Catholic, but singing was stronger in the Escamilla family than differences in religious ideology. When we saw Tio Daniel, we knew that we were in trouble. It did not take long before mother was notified, and I was in trouble again after my Uncle Daniel spilled the beans. There were definite reasons why my mother consistently kept an eye on me.

Despite the distance, the family always stayed in touch with other family members in Mexico. Uncles Roberto and Santiago Escamilla, my mother's brothers who lived in Monterrey, would come to see us often, and we would go to see them, too. Every time Uncle Roberto came, we would have the opportunity to sing with him. He knew a lot of Mexican songs from the golden age of Mexican vernacular music. At least twice a year, we would go to Villaldama (dad's birthplace) and Sabinas Hidalgo (mom's birthplace) to visit family.

Those who would come from my father's side to work with us were undocumented. As a child, it never occurred to me that they were not documented. Tio Gregorio lived near us. I remember that after working long hours he would come and grab the guitar and sing some *corridos* (ballads). My mother loved them all, and it was clear that she tried to protect Tio Gollo more than her other brothers because of his kindness, generosity, and lack of defenses. He needed to be protected. My father was one who always protected him, and Tio Gollo appreciated and respected my father, though at times he was afraid of him. Speaking of my father, he played a major role in both families, but that came with certain conditions. The biggest one was his colorful language. Being tall, strong, and very certain of himself, my father stood above anyone else as he spoke with this colorful language. The word *chingao* has many variations; not every word means the same. Words like *chingar*, *chingon*, and *chingaderas*, once again, all have different meanings.

My father used all these and other words eloquently. Later in life we learned that dad was part Jewish. Although my other uncles (Roberto and Santiago) were far more formally educated and middle-class (and we were not at the time), they could never escape the presence of Dad. He was the man of his word!

I had an incredible mother. Much of her life she spent in the kitchen since she had to feed three meals to ten to fifteen people daily. For all the work she had to do, she never complained. She would get up to start the day around four thirty in the morning, every morning of the week. She knew which two Spanish radio stations (Del Rio and San Antonio) were available at the time, and she would listen to them. She would sing along as she prepared breakfast. It was a joy to hear her as she went about preparing the daily food and singing beautiful Mexican songs. I remember one day during our very early years of marriage, Norma and I stayed with them overnight. My wife, never an early riser, heard Mama singing. She turned to me and asked what time it was, and I told her that it was five fifteen in the morning. She was floored. An hour later Mama arrived with hot chocolate since it was Norma's favorite. My mother loved to cook, and she thoroughly enjoyed seeing others eating the food that she made. Nothing satisfied her more than cooking for others, often in massive amounts.

When I was dating Norma, I would drive monthly from the Rio Grande Valley to Mama's house, stay overnight, and then on Saturday visit Norma in San Antonio. Mama was always ready to send her and her folks some of the food that they liked. So I was the carrier and messenger, and I would bring a car full of *atole de arroz* (rice pudding), cornbread, eggs, and homemade cheese. Frankly, I was somewhat embarrassed. I felt that I was buying Norma and her family for my benefit. Neither Norma's family nor my mother paid much attention to this feeling, and I kept shipping and carrying good food.

The Villarreal family was more serious, tough, not overly musical, and short on humor. One of my father's traits was his inability to openly express love or emotion. I think my father felt that being emotional made him weak and vulnerable, and that was unacceptable. This is very much part of our culture, particularly if you are male and the head of a family. In external affairs he was the leader of the pack, and I guess he had the obligation of putting a strong face on for the family and the community. Dad was mostly expressive, charming, charismatic, and boisterous. But on a personal basis, he would share very few thoughts, and he certainly was not complimentary. I don't think that my father ever congratulated me or anyone else for accomplishments. Instead, he would brag about our accomplishments to friends and community members. Unquestionably, he loved and cared for us.

Anglos in our community were careful when they dealt with my father. To some he was a threat. Dad had the ability to act humble and dumb. It was a good act. For example, when Dad bought an eighty-acre plot of land, it had no great value other than for farming. This changed in a matter of three years. When the former owner of this piece of land learned that oil had been discovered at Dad's farm, he returned in hopes of buying back the land. He offered four times the value of the eighty acres with the understanding that the land where the house was would remain Dad's property. Oil or no oil, Dad would not sell the land. As the story goes, Dad and Mom always dreamed of having a place for themselves since in their lifetime they had owned no land or house. After much wrangling, the guy left and never returned. When Dad bought this farm, it was financed by a person from Karnes City. When Dad finished paying for the property, he asked for a new loan to buy another piece of land. Once again, he paid the money that he borrowed for the new land on time. Soon after, a family from the community put their land for sale since they were moving to San Antonio. The same guy who financed the eighty-acre plot of land came to our house to see if Dad wanted to purchase the land. It was a tough decision for my parents. They certainly wanted to buy more land, but they would have to mortgage the land they had and that was troublesome. With a mortgage the potential for losing the property was there. Soon after, they both decided to let it go. The Hinojosa farm was sold to somebody else.

Dad took full responsibility to prepare us to be good farmers and ranchers. He knew his world and he wanted to pass it to us. But Dad was worried that we were neither prepared nor had the skills to succeed. I was convinced that none of us could ever match Dad's will, skill, and strength! This was certainly true of myself. I gave my father major concerns because my ranching and farming skills were limited. I failed in the tasks of being a good farmer and rancher. I think that I had the guts but not the desire. My dreams were never, ever shared with anyone. I felt that if I communicated my thoughts, I would alienate my mother and father, and that was the last thing I wanted to do.

As a farmer and rancher, Dad was a formidable master. He could be a veterinarian as well as a good cowboy. Once again, I was neither. Dad castrated pigs, sheep, and young bulls, and he did it with style. When the time came that we needed meat, he would kill the animal, skin it, and butcher it for Mom to use in the kitchen. But he did more, purposely involving me in these affairs. Killing an animal was done by cutting its throat. I had the responsibility to hold the animal's head so he could perform his duty. I would hold my head and turn my eyes elsewhere so I could not see what was about to happen. I would stand there holding the animal's head, ready to put the episode behind me, but it was not that easy. Dad would stop and direct me to look at what I was doing and watch his performance. I did it against my will. Boy, for Dad, this was a disappointing act.

Besides my immediate family, other members of our family lived with us. My Uncle Pancho Montalbo lived with us his entire life. He married my mother's sister, Sara, but unfortunately, she passed away when she gave birth to my cousin Remijio at the age of 20. Remijio grew up with us since childhood, and he was like a brother to us. We also lived with Jesús Flores, who also grew up with us along with his father, Atilano Flores. Guadalupe and Saturnina were dad's sisters who never married. Both lived with us. His third sister, Cruz, married Tio Gollo, my mother's brother. Within the confines of our home, I had many aunts and uncles and sundry other characters from Mexico who ultimately stayed there. Our cousins Arturo and Hector were born in the United States, but during the 1930s the US government repatriated their family back to Mexico. When they were in their teens, their parents sent them to live with us, and they were with us until they were married. My other cousin, Beto Santos, also came from Mexico and lived with us for several years before he moved to Houston, where he started a restaurant. There were other family members that would come and stay with us to harvest the crops during the summer and fall, including Uncles Cecilio, Pedro, Cesario, Juan, David, and Manuel and two other family members whose names I don't remember. More than thirty people lived under two small roofs next to each other out in the country. My father would deal with all aspects of life outside the home, and my mother, with the assistance of my father's sister Lupita, would take care of the internal responsibilities of the house. My parents were compatible and inseparable.

My mother took full responsibility for all matters relating to our home, including raising all of us and feeding many people. Mother took care of disciplinary matters, and she did a masterful job. Besides taking the responsibility to produce three square meals a day in a home situation without running water, electricity, or a refrigerator, and with only a wood-burning stove and a wood window in the kitchen, my mother made miracles on a dirt floor. My mother and my sisters washed all the clothes by hand and kept a clean house. We were never hungry or dirty.

When I was growing up, the women at home did all the cooking, cleaning, ironing, and other household chores. No men or boys were involved in these essential tasks. When food was ready, we were called in and sat around the table; we enjoyed the meal, and we walked out of the dining room without lifting a finger. The women took care of cleaning and washing the dishes. This has many important implications in life. When I was at home, it never occurred to me the enormous struggles that women had to go through, including cooking, cleaning, washing clothes, and many other household duties, plus working outside harvesting crops. It was not until I started cooking and got away from that environment that I came to a full realization of what my poor mother and my sisters and the many women of the world had to go through to survive. They cooked three square meals a day in the most difficult circumstances. Typically, there were twelve to fourteen people eating at any one time at home. Moreover, when we were ready to go back to the fields to work, my sisters joined us until the evening, when, once again, they would join my mother to finalize the dinner and clean up after the meal. Unfortunately, it was a way of life, and little if nothing was said about it. The next day, the whole process was repeated.

My mother revealed a talent for subtleties and a reward system unmatched by anyone that I have known. She was loved, respected, and admired. Often things would get done quietly, without her lifting a finger. My mother had considerable compassion for those who suffered and struggled in life. She had a great devotion to helping anyone who needed her, even beyond her family. Because of her generosity, members of our community responded accordingly with love and respect for her efforts. She had power, and she used it with finesse. She knew it, and she pursued multiple causes for her family. Dad shared a similar compassion for the less fortunate, and he followed my mother's example in sharing resources. Throughout their lives they helped, fed, and comforted hundreds upon hundreds of people, including members of our immediate and extended family. Mom's moral commitment and perseverance were unquestionable. On the surface Dad was a macho man, but inside he had a softness that he didn't want people to know about. My mother was focused, quiet, and subtle with a benign demeanor. I am proud to claim that my brothers and sisters carry on those traits with great enthusiasm.

I am fortunate to have had good brothers and sisters. As the youngest of my siblings, I always looked to them for guidance, but at the same time I took them for granted. I saw them as older people, although our ages were not radically different. I was in my own world and paid little attention to them. Hortensia was highly intelligent with great abilities to perform any kind of activities performed by men or women. She could ride horses and drive tractors, and she was a great cook. She was kind, tough, thoughtful, and well disciplined. Unfortunately, she was accustomed to a tradition in which women took second place, despite her abilities and leadership qualities. She played a significant role in the development of my family. It was a great tragedy for us to lose her at a young age. My brother José Gonzalo was the second child of our family. I got to know him better since he lived far longer than most of my older siblings. Like Hortensia, Gonzalo was most instrumental to our family. He was a bright, kind, generous, compassionate, and lovable human being. He was not a soft person. He was tough, courageous, and protective of our family. This continued to be true when he became the father of seven children. I interacted with him on many occasions and under many different circumstances, and we never had difficulty with each other. Instead, it was always respect, love, and admiration; he was a great compadre! Each of us was different, and Olga, the third child, was different than my two other siblings. Whatever limitations Olga had, she replaced with an enormous amount of courage, determination, and diligence. She was astute and ambitious, and her ambition was to raise a family that would not suffer as much as she did. Olga did a magnificent job in preparing her children for life. She raised four kids, and they are the best.

Oralia, the fourth child, has lived longer than any member of my family, and she has always had the knack to take center stage. When my mother died, my sister Oralia was single, living at home with Dad and my sister Minerva. For her it was natural that she would take command of the family. She had much in common with Dad, and he was very pleased that Lala was in charge. Totally devoted to the family, Lala was tough, direct, no-nonsense, and very straight in her dealings. She was controversial since she would take positions that were not popular with the family and community. Ultimately, she married a great guy, Lauro, and they had a great marriage. Currently, Lala is at a nursing home in Kenedy. Her husband passed away several years ago.

The fifth child was Epifanio Jr. Since we were closer in age, we had the opportunity to play together when we were growing up.

He was genial, kind, carefree, and funny, but due to illness he had a difficult childhood. Epifanio and I loved each other, but at an early age we took different paths. He married Maria Espinoza and had seven children. Unable to adequately survive on the farm, he departed with his family, looking for a better place to live. He found the right place in Florida. He and Maria raised seven wonderful children.

During my childhood, Minerva was closest to me since we were only a year apart. Since my curiosity often ran away with me, invariably I would get in trouble with my mother. Minerva would try her best to protect me. As a child I always thought that I had a handle on her. That would last until my mother would get on her high horse and punish me for my wrong doings. Although Minerva and Oralia were together all the time, Minerva was different, causing pain to Oralia and Dad. Socially, Minerva had greater admiration for the Anglo style of life. Throughout this time, socially, Anglos were more liberals than Mexican Americans. For example, Minerva wanted to use shorts during the summer, and Dad refused to accept her wishes. Dad was a traditional man, and shorts at home for women was a scandal. Tension was consistently present. Ultimately, she married an old Anglo, against Dad's wishes. Things got better and Minerva got her wish. More important, her life was more in tune as she married and lived comfortably for the rest of her life.

As family we were no different than most Mexican American families. We suffered similar consequences in the hands of the Anglo community. Mexican Americans had much in common as a group, but unifying against the Anglo for a better life was a thing of the future. So for generations life never changed much. Victimization came in various forms. To begin with, we were conquered by Anglos creating an environment of segregation, discrimination, racism, and humiliation; local and state laws were passed protecting the conquerors against Mexicans; for the most part, our culture, language, and traditions were unacceptable; to obtain a formal education was almost impossible; wages for Mexican American workers were low and never increasing; the power of the vote was years away; and owning property and a house was still a dream. Once again, these conditions existed for generations. However, during my generation things began to change, and there was some light at the end of the tunnel. The generation of my nieces and nephews changed the situation. Like many Latinos we became middle-class. Life became more complete but still not equitable with the Anglo community. Considerable changes begin to occur, creating stronger communities as our voices increased in the name of justice and equality.

For years I have been told to write about the world that we lived in since little has been written. My world comprised people of Mexican origin and Anglos, constituting a conflicting and difficult past characterized by superiority/inferiority relationships and the subordination of Mexicans.

When we compare ourselves with Anglos, we see a different migratory path, from south to north, as opposed to from the Northeast to the Southwest. This south-to-north migration pattern has been in existence since before the landing at Plymouth Rock. We were here before Anglos came to the Southwest, and we were mestizos (mixed-race identities between Spaniards and Indigenous people). This change is exemplified in our literature, among many other things. One only needs to look at the publications in the *Southwestern Historical Quarterly* to see the difference. Article and book reviews found in the *Quarterly* reflect a more revisionist take on history than ever before. For example, book reviews, a major component of the *Quarterly*, have been more diversified in content, reflecting the demography of Texas. Both Anglos and Latinos have contributed much to the historical literature of our two vigorous cultures in recent years.

My departure and transition from a rural environment and strong family unit to a world of academic life had the great potential to expand into a new culture at the expense of leaving behind the culture that I grew up with. But as I became more assimilated and integrated into the political system via academics, my identity of being of Mexican origin strengthened. At this stage of development, I was not about to get lost and become fully Americanized. To the contrary, as I became more American, I also became more Mexican. It really pushed me to become a bicultural and bilingual educator. I attribute this phenomenon to three factors. First, I had lived my entire life in South Texas, an area rich in Mexican culture. Second, most of my professional life was spent in metropolitan areas on the border between the United States and Mexico. The third factor is my wife, Norma. My Spanish vocabulary and writing skills extended over the years. She served as a connection with her Mexican family living in Mexico. On several occasions I have written articles in Spanish for Mexican journals. I could have learned the language better earlier in life, but the opportunity was not there. I had no formal education in the Spanish language, and nothing was available.

Gradually, by the twenty-first century, many obstacles have been removed. Latinos continue to integrate in great numbers, and the economic and social differences are fading out. More than ever Anglos in our community need to be part of the Mexican American people. I think that many want to be part of us. But the path to seek this closeness contradicts a long tradition of Anglos being on their own. I contend that many Anglos would prefer the status quo, but the environment has changed and it has become impossible to be isolated. In some ways Anglos are not as competitive, and they are outnumbered. Seeking closeness to Mexican Americans has become essential and beneficial. Take the school districts in South Texas: The demography has changed, and Mexican American students greatly outnumber Anglos. Meanwhile, the administration and teachers, for the most part, are still Anglos. Anglos have the great need to rely on Mexican Americans for their survival. The Latino community accepts the relationship since it is beneficial to them too. The world keeps changing, and as it changes Anglos have the necessity and, perhaps, the desire to yield to the Latino community. Economically and educationally, among other factors, both groups have the necessity to coexist. Coexistence creates greater coexistence!

This background and relationship continue to influence my outlook on life and provide a constant reminder to broaden my world so I can see the beauty of life in greater depth and to reach the unreachable goal—namely, to earn a doctorate. When I first taught in higher education, it was at a new community college approximately forty miles from where I was born. I was hired at the insistence of my high school superintendent, who at the time was a newly elected member of the college board. This was the same person who four years earlier, in 1963, had denied me a position at the high school because "the school board was not ready hire a Mexican American to teach students in high school." This, by the way, was not an isolated case.

Although for years I had the passion to write these accounts and make comparisons between then and now, I never did. But the time has come to see the major transformation of these two dominant cultures characterized by their ethnic relations, these cultures who need each other and have the desire and necessity to work together. Despite the need for interdependence in our relationships, some measure of social distance continue to exist. The situation is further exacerbated by the presence of ignorance, distrust, indifference, and misunderstanding, as well as the maintenance of superiority and inferiority complexes in certain social and political circles.

The time has come to address current issues and live new dimensions since there have been many changes in the past two generations. The alienation, discrimination, and lack of understanding of our political culture has changed in the past two generations. As stated earlier, the Anglo community has greater necessity to accept our culture. A political and historical analysis of bridging the two cultures makes a clear statement: The greater the social justice, the greater the opportunity and involvement in our social and familial relations. This makes for a more productive and equal society that benefits everyone, including minorities who have been historically marginalized.

It is within the confines of these institutions (starting with the family) that I have been able to learn to understand the meaning and purpose of life as it existed and from there try to reach new horizons. I have tried and will try every way possible to reach the reader to explain this unique and complex journey of more than two generations, a journey that in many ways we all share as cultural beings. Additionally, there is a need to expand the literary works of people of Mexican origin in this region. The Chicano literature has expended since the 1970s and thereafter. Nevertheless, the scholarship in this area, as the subtitle of this memoir indicates, "from a field worker to a university professor," is still open to good books. Historically, Latino culture has magnified the oral part of relating these stories as they are experienced, but they have not been documented in writing. Yet there are many areas of our literature that have not touched the real significance of our culture and history. The issue here is that there is so much territory to cover and not enough time. It is unfortunate that *nuestra gente* (our people) have not taken the opportunity to put in writing the many important and colorful stories of their lives, stories that, I am certain, our new generation would like to read. But I must grant that writings of *la vida cotidiana* (the life of common folks) are complex and interesting. So the intent of this book is to throw a ray of light on this historical journey and the stories of the many that have lived in South Texas for generations. Chapter 4 will devote time to discussing the many paradoxes that exist between public schools and the Mexican American family, since this is the world that captured my imagination.

Chapter 4

The Paradox of School and the Mexican American Family

The nature of our social environment contributed greatly to our failure to learn and move up. The rejection of our culture and language in conjunction with an intense level of discrimination was completed without any fanfare and without a word being said. This was part of the assimilation and acculturation process, and it made it almost impossible to assimilate and acculturate to the ethos of the school system. Words like *discrimination*, *racism*, *segregation*, and *inequality* were not part of the vocabulary in the school system or in the Anglo community. We lived in a world where these "isms" did not exist, and since we were so accustomed to this culture, we accepted it without questions.

At school I had a lot of company from family members and friends. At Cadillac Elementary my brother Epifanio, sister Minerva, and two of my double cousins were with me and we were in the same grade. It should be noted that regardless of the student's age, we were put in the same class and same grade. We often discussed matters related to school, although none of us had a good handle on it, and neither did our parents. We were a group of students working outside the system with no guidance, assistance, or knowledge; we were not recognized for our cultural and linguistic differences, and anti-Mexican sentiment was rampant and out of control. It was a total disconnect since our parents were totally absent from the educational system, and their presence and political influence was practically nonexistent. There were two separate worlds: Mexican American families and the educational system. Everything related to schools seemed to be accidental, uncoordinated, and hopeless. Our parents were probably aware but felt powerless to do anything. Mexican American people in their dealings with Anglos tried not to cause any trouble because it meant punishment. That being the case, the Anglos took a forward look and did what was beneficial for them without any major concern for other groups. They also knew there was little we could do about it. We were obligated to attend school until the age of 16, after which we worked full-time in the fields. In the novel *George Washington Gomez*, Americo Paredes gives an account on parental struggles in their exertions for their children to succeed in education often under most difficult circumstances.

My first real encounter with public schools was at around the age of 7. Cadillac Elementary was a four-room wooden-frame building in the southern part of Karnes County, Texas, approximately four miles northeast of Pawnee and four miles southeast of where we lived. Attending Cadillac Elementary had some benefits since we did not have to work in the fields, and it served as a meeting place to visit others and play. Going to this rural school was the first time we became part of the Anglo world. For kids that wanted to assimilate, the school presented opportunities and attractions. Although I wanted to go to school, the drudgery of the classroom setting was difficult to endure. With our limited understanding of the English language and the little attention given to us, it was mind-numbing. The only salvation was recess and going to the bathroom, which was about two hundred yards away. Believe me, in going to the outhouse, we slowed our steps to kill time. We were bored and frustrated. Diversity as we know it today was not part of the traditional school system, at least not for Mexican American students.

Our transportation to and from school was an old 1935 International bus that failed to function many times during the year. An old Anglo man was the school bus driver. In my early years of schooling, the bus would only come to the El Oso Store, approximately a mile and a half from home. We would walk every morning to catch the bus there, and in the afternoon we were dropped off at the same place. Sometimes, the bus would not arrive for whatever reason, so the day would turn into a working day out in the fields. The sitting arrangements on the school bus were intentionally designed to segregate whites from Mexicans. The bus had four long seats. In the middle of those four rows there was a heavy frame wire to separate us. We often talked to each other across the metal wires. Much later, we had a new bus that resembled the buses that we have today, but segregation continued. Anglos sat in the back of the bus, and we sat at the front. There was an imaginary line that served to divide the two groups, and no one violated it except one time.

One day my cousin Chindo and I decided to sit in the back of the bus in hopes that it would ultimately break this unwanted segregation. We were one of the first to get on the bus, so we took the back seat and waited to see what would happen. Well, we soon found out. Two big and beefy Anglo kids, Benny and Louis, asked us to move to the front. We refused. Without hesitation they grabbed us, and we were shoved back where we "belonged." Stanley Bergman, the bus driver and high school principal, appeared not to notice. When we arrived at school, I told him what had happened. He told me that he would visit with the superintendent. He never came back with an answer. At this point in time, I decided that I was creating problems that I could not solve.

The four-room school had four teachers, one of them the principal of the school. My twelve years in elementary school were the most unproductive years of my entire educational experience. Young, innocent, and ignorant, I could not see the light at the end of the tunnel; knowing neither the English language nor the culture of the school, I had a frustrating experience. The first teacher that I had was Lillian Monson. Lillian probably had no more than a high school education.

She had little respect for the students, and she loved to reprimand us whenever she had the opportunity.

For example, one day we were heading home on the bus, which made a stop for one of the students. Before the bus came to a full stop, a girl got up to walk toward the front of the bus. Another student next to me moved his leg in front of her, and she tumbled to the floor. The driver asked who had done it, and the student next to me pointed toward me. The driver asked for my name, and he proceeded to report me the following day. When I arrived at school the following day, Lillian Monson was waiting for me. Her mode of punishment was simple: She locked me in the closet and left me there all day. No water, no food, no nothing. I managed well, except when I needed to use the bathroom; that was a real problem. I was so embarrassed to face the students. I never told my parents, and life went on.

I met Stanley Bergman when I first went to Cadillac school as a first grader. We spent sixteen years together (twelve years in Cadillac Elementary and four years at Pawnee High School. As time went on, Mr. Bergman asked me if I was willing to practice running in preparation to run in school relays. Why he asked me was beyond my comprehension. I was older than the rest of the students, my grades were low, and there were Anglo students that were far better runners than me. Even as a kid, I was puzzled. To choose a Mexican American who was in elementary school to run with high school students in regional relays during the spring season was totally unusual. What was in me that attracted his attention? I do not know! Of course, I liked the idea and the attention that I was getting, so I took his word and started running. This was the scenario: I would ride the school bus the whole route until everybody was gone. We then returned to the school, and I would practice running. At times he would clock me or film me while I was running. After more than an hour of working out, he would drive me home in his old 1953 Ford car. When it came time to running in the relay, Bergman and his buddy Jess Philips, the elementary principal at Pawnee, would take me to participate in regional track meets to run the mile. I guess that something was coming along the way that I did not know. This incident in my school life had great importance. I begin to have greater appreciation of going to school; I was being accepted despite the circumstances at that time; and I continued running for a long time until recently, when I could not run any longer. Walking became part of my exercise after I could not run. I certainly enjoy a good walk every day.

For most of my family and friends that attended public schools in the 1930s and 1940s, the school was segregated. Typically, there were two schools: One was made out of brick, and the other was made out of wood. The brick building had four rooms, and the wood building had one room. One was on one side of the road, and the other was on the other side. You can guess in which of the two building the Mexican Americans attended. My older brother and sisters went to the wooden school for about four years before dropping out. I was at the tail end of this cycle. By the time I started school, they had integrated Anglos and Mexican Americans, though not Black students; they had to find a way to attend a Black school in Kenedy, fifteen miles away, and their segregation continued into the 1950s.

At Cadillac the classroom was divided into two parts. One side of the room was for Anglos, and the other side was for us. The Anglo section had one seat per student, while our side had church pews. One long seat would be occupied by eight to ten students. We called our side *la marranera* (a pig pen). Typically, we sat there like wooden logs, frustrated by the inactivity. Most of the class's attention and activity was for the Anglos, presumably because they could read and write. The rest of us served as observers, and we were bored to death. On one occasion my brother, sister, and cousins were sitting *en la marranera*, waiting for the bell to ring. It must have been around eleven in the morning, and I was getting hungry. Being bored and having nothing else to do, I wrote a note to my brother in Spanish. In the note I told my brother the ultimate breakfast that my mother knew how to cook: homemade flour tortillas, chorizo with eggs, fresh baked beans, fried potatoes, and a fresh glass of milk (I meant fresh milk directly from the cow). Mr. Bergman noticed that I was passing a note to my brother, so he asked me to turn it in to him. I felt embarrassed and terrified. He was oblivious as to the contents. He called Art Treviño, a more assimilated Tejano student, to read the letter before the class. So what was the big deal? Under normal circumstances I would have been proud of my culture. It was just a recipe for a good breakfast. But for a small child under circumstances in which being Mexican was not accepted, it created an ordeal. It is too bad to have a teacher insensitive to students and able to humiliate a student. This behavior can have long-ranging consequences, even causing students who need education the most to drop out of school. But I was stubborn, and there was no way I was going to drop out. And this was in a culture in which being Mexican was not socially acceptable at school.

Our main goal at school was to play on the school grounds, which is natural for children. As soon as Mr. Gilley, our elementary school principal, walked from his house to the school, the bell would ring and we would follow him to the classroom. But when he rang the bell in our classroom, we were on our way to have fun no matter what. To my recollection there was far more integration of the two groups on the playground than in our classroom. We learned little in the classroom, despite the teachers' efforts. Perhaps more importantly, we were learning how to get along with each other. There was nothing there that resembled inclusiveness, and the outlook of the teachers and the administration was traditional. The gap between cultures was very wide, and the bridges to link one culture with the other did not exist at this stage of development.

The origin of this small, rural school was foreign to us. But as far as formal education is concerned, the ambience was very unsettling and remote. It was a mere necessity to be there, as required by state law. Looking back, I realize that many administrators and teachers looked forward to the time when the Mexican students would reach the age at which they would drop out of school. Most people understood this phenomenon, and life just went on without any considerations or questions. We were in a state of silence, and to speak out meant trouble.

It would be years before the voices of the Latinos would rise. But even during this period of our history (1940 to 1970s), there were proactive challenges to the socioeconomic circumstances that we were living. A prime example for fighting desegregation in Texas was the *Delgado v. Bastrop* case, where the court ruling was in favor of ending legal segregation of Mexican Americans in Texas. There were other court cases developing to counter desegregation. Unfortunately, de facto segregation did not parallel with de jure segregation.

The impact of this school culture on a rural environment created a split personality on just about anyone. There were two cultures with minimal overlap. At home, like my family members, I was talkative, noisy, expressive, and vocal. I enjoyed the world of Mexican music; I wanted to be a singer, and I could not wait to get older so I could join the activities of my two older brothers that I loved. To counter this cultural environment was the school system. My social behavior changed dramatically when I was there. I was shy, quiet, very subordinate, unassuming, and a very "nice kid." It was a world of "yes, sir" and "no, sir," never challenging authority. I did not like this at all, but, right or wrong, I accepted that role to survive. Perhaps I was unaware, but there was something telling me that I was looking at a long road and that this behavior would take me on since being a normal child would not work. If there were other options, I was completely unaware. I chose a new road, and in the long run, it made a great difference.

At the end of my first year at Pawnee, I graduated from junior high in a class of about thirteen students. Unfortunately, it was common in those years for a lot of Mexican Americans to drop out of school. During those years finishing middle school was considered the end of formal schooling. My cousin Chindo, like several other Mexican Americans, did not return to school following graduation from middle school. Although he had passed to the ninth grade, the first year of high school, he had no desire to continue. As far as he was concerned, he had completed his term, and he wanted out. In late August he told me that he was ready to tell his parents that he was not going to school any longer. I presumed that it would not be a difficult task to convince them since the family was not focused on formal schooling. He tried to persuade me to join him since that meant staying together as a duet in our pursuit of becoming singers and musicians, but I was not ready. By this time I was set to tackle secondary education, and I was excited about it. Yet it bothered me considerably to let him go since Chindo and I were first cousins twice, we were close friends, we were almost the same age, and we both loved music. On top of all these good relations, Chindo was the clown of the family, producing a whole lot of humor. From that point on, I was on my own. I had very few close friends, a lot of acquaintances, and, as far as I knew, no enemies. All my brothers, sisters, cousins, and friends were out in the field working, while I spent most of my time trying to figure out a path that would take me to graduate from high school. My hope was that I could finish high school before my 22nd birthday. It would be great, although there was considerable uncertainty. This dream I was not ready to share.

My parents deeply believed in education, but under the circumstances it made it impossible to fulfill this obligation, yet they would not stop us from learning. To the contrary, my parents' effort to learn was consistent throughout the years. Here is a prime example: Our parents taught us how to read and write in Spanish even though no books were available at home. In my case, my parents made a connection with a friend and neighbor who was willing and knowledgeable to assist. Abundio Chapa was an older, self-educated man who was blind. He had a great appreciation for education. He lived with his wife and his sons. Seledina (La China) made a living by cleaning the Lynch's (the *patrón*) two-story home. Their house, near the *patrón* house, was far smaller, but they had a tiny library with around ten or fifteen geography and history books. After school and on the weekends, I would visit him and read to him, and he would correct me as I went along. He called me Betito, for Roberto. My world of Spanish expanded, and I am thankful. One day while we were discussing the future, he told me that there was a possibility that I could become a lawyer. For the first time in my life somebody brought to my attention that I could become a lawyer, a profession. I kept this idea for a long time, and though I never became a lawyer, I achieved another profession.

Neither of my parents participated in any school functions. It was not until I graduated from high school, sixteen years later, that my parents were able to attend. It seemed clear to them that the nature of the schools was for someone else. Besides, it was common for all the family members to work starting at the early age of 5 or 6. Family members of different ages had different responsibilities. Therefore, education was totally secondary in terms of surviving as a family unit. Staying away from the school had its own benefits. It was a way to avoid direct discrimination and stay out of trouble.

In the early years when I was attending elementary school at Cadillac, the disdain for anything Mexican was dominant and overwhelming. This pattern of behavior was common in Texas and the Southwest, though particularly in South Texas. Looking back at the history of the Southwest, the level of discrimination in South Texas was far more pronounced than anywhere else in the Southwest. Moreover, now, after much studying and reading on this subject, it is easy to conclude that South Texas was home to the worst historical relationships between Mexican Americans and Anglos than any other part of this nation. Culturally, South Texas is very much part of the South. Southern immigrants who came to this area came to expand slavery, and the Mexican population became part of that culture. It was a social calamity that lasted for generations, and it was a significant factor in the school system since schools are the most important agents of acculturation and assimilation. The influence of the South continues to be part of this region, and we continue to have a variation of social problems.

Part of this Southern culture created a social environment in which Spanish became a foreign language, and, therefore, it came to be prohibited in the school system and other areas of government. A state law that prohibited the use of the Spanish language on school grounds was based on the idea that if we stopped speaking our native language, then we would learn English. I am certain that the legislative body that designated and passed this law was thinking far more about dominance than education. We were constantly reminded that Spanish was prohibited in spite our great difficulty trying to speak and understand English. Our integration to a different culture via schools was truncated and difficult to adjust to. There was no road that would take us from one language to another. To the contrary, we were socially condemned because of our heavy accents when speaking English. We were criticized for our "unwillingness" to assimilate, and we were discriminated against and ostracized when we tried to integrate. We were even critiqued on the way we spoke Spanish because it was not Castilian. The principals and teachers did not know our language and culture, and there was no evidence that they wanted to learn it, even though they lived in a bastion of Mexican American culture.

There was nothing in the school system that reflected our culture except our presence. For children who were proud of their parents and culture, the educational system instilled in us a desire to walk out of the school system as soon as we could. The lack of cultural toleration was applied even to the food we ate. Take, for example, eating tortillas; there was a tradition and unwritten rule at Cadillac not to eat tortillas on the school grounds or in front of Anglos. This was considered an affront to others in this environment. Eating tortillas was demeaning and socially unacceptable. On the other hand, if you brought white bread and bologna or other varieties of processed meat, you were with the rest of the dominant bunch, so there was no problem. It is understandable why people of Mexican origin were resentful and angry. So when it was lunchtime, those of us who brought tortillas for lunch would automatically walk off the school grounds to the small *arroyo* (creek) nearby to eat our food before returning to the school grounds. This went on for years. I sometimes felt that my mother should pack me lunch with white bread and bologna and join the dominant culture, but there was no bologna or white bread at home. One of the important manifestations from the past has been to resist the invasion of another culture upon us. Resistance against the encroachment of other cultures has been a pattern throughout the years. This was certainly the case of eating tortillas.

Stubbornly, at this stage of development, I began to realize that I needed to do two things that sometimes seemed impossible for a child. First, I would assimilate, and second, I would preserve my native culture and language. This became a lifelong effort. It took a long time to accomplish this feat since I had to expand in both cultural directions. It has been a considerable accomplishment, particularly when I wanted to follow the tradition of my devoted parents, who sacrificed to pass on to us a strong culture with dignity and respect.

For past generations (from the 1840s to the 1930s), Anglos made a concerted effort to eliminate our culture, or if not, at least to contain it. As we know, this feat was impossible to accomplish. It was not an option. We must remember that the Spaniards established deep roots in this hemisphere; the Mexicans continued to support the underpinnings of this culture; and the Indigenous culture melted with Spaniards and Mexicans to create a powerful mestizo culture well established in the Southwest. When we ran into ethnic difficulties, our parents and grandparents always reminded us that we were here first and our land was, literally, stolen by whites. It was an expression of anger and frustration that often went nowhere. The culture of South Texas and the Southwest is rooted in the Mexican culture. On the surface our culture is Anglo. The power and presence of Anglos as well as the overpowering use of technology covered the roots of the Mexican culture. Yet as time moves on, the Mexican culture continues to surface and rise. Is that what I want? Not necessarily, but this is what time and experience have shown us.

Throughout my professional career, I have been involved in conversations with all kinds of people, particularly people that labor hard to earn a meal. These discussions have been about the struggle to overcome major obstacles and barriers in our daily lives. We always ended our conversations with humor and counting our blessings for having wonderful parents and ancestors. Since early in life I have wondered what we were doing and what we are leaving behind for others to follow. In my world practically every professional movement means breaking with the past and seeking new ground. In the world that I grew up in, we often looked at the future with little or no guidance and understanding, but now this is changing.

In my early years, social, political, and educational institutions were dominated by groups who were indifferent or who failed to recognize and acknowledge the plight of people of Mexican origin. They were unwilling or unable to learn from us or to understand the struggles of people with a different culture and language, thus hindering our development. Historically, whites have been fearful of Mexicans and Mexico, which is one of the many reasons why Mexicans are so stereotyped. Such notions as being dirty, violent, drug-consumed, and exotic have been common for years but is something that has changed in our current generation. What are things that influence fear? The number of Latinos has surpassed the number of white people in Texas; jobs that were once obtained by Anglos have diminished and have been given to Latinos; and the mere color of skin can be threatening. This does not mean that they are bad people, not at all! But ignorance, bigotry, and discrimination complicate matters considerably. Today, many members of the Anglo community have a strong desire for closeness and work together for common interests. On the other hand, Latinos are not far away from being fearful of Anglos, even though it is less now than it used to be.

It is certainly not my intent to dwell on the discriminatory institutions that we dealt with daily versus the culture and values of my family. These are two important and distinct factors that have had a significant impact on my personal life and my professional career, in South Texas and elsewhere. It has impacted my personal behavior and thinking in ways that are hard to imagine. It was not until I gave it a lot of thought and perspective that I was able to partially realize how my life and behavior were carved out of these circumstances and the relations between two different cultural groups. Sometimes, it is painful to account for these life experiences since they come from an era of considerable obscurity and sacrifice. The essence of the pain caused involves the denial of human dignity, respect, justice, and opportunity, particularly for my parents, my family, and generations past. Via these writings, I am trying to define and bridge the gap between home and school, from one extreme as an overaged elementary student to the other extreme of becoming a university professor. I am most fortunate to be part of this great transformation of the political culture of the Mexican American people, once considered inferior by others, now an integrated, robust, and young group that can act and work side by side with other groups to make this country even stronger.

Yet despite many gains, the social, economic, and educational gap continues to exist as we continue to bridge it. Richard Parker's book *Lone Star Nation* defines this transformation: "But now, just into the second decade of the 21st century, Texas was in the throes of sweeping and fundamental change: economic change, population change, demographic change—almost 200 years of Anglo dominance were yielding to an ever-increasing Hispanic population."[1] Although we are part of this transformation, we still have a ways to go.

By accident and not by design, I have had the opportunity to teach at all levels of the public educational system: elementary, middle, and high school, as well as at a community college and two universities, teaching both undergraduate and graduate students. For the most part, however, my professional life has been in higher education, first as a community college instructor and then as a university professor and administrator at a major university for thirty years. After these long and enriching experiences, I moved back to a place near where I grew up to enjoy the fruits of life and my family, to travel, read, write, teach, and participate as an activist and scholar in the gradual transformation of the political culture of South Texas. Since retiring I have continued to teach at San Antonio College and the University of Texas at San Antonio. After more than sixty-two years of teaching, I finally retired the fall semester of 2024.

Our biggest problem, as far as we were concerned, was our inability to appreciate and comprehend the environment that we were in or the learning process. As far as I can tell, there was no attempt by leaders in the school system to bridge the gap between the two groups. I assume they thought their group was on the right track, and, therefore, our group had to make all the adjustments. After all, this is America! Moreover, there was a long tradition of Latinos dropping out early, so it was more of the same. In this environment all we knew was that we were less than. We were uncomfortable and frustrated, but we had to behave as expected. We knew that the teachers and administrators were Anglos and on the side of the Anglos. That was clear. On the other hand, if our parents learned that we were causing trouble, they would come after us. We were boxed in, so we learned to stay low, abide by the rules, and get out of any kind of trouble so we could stay in school.

For the most part, our parents saw the rule of law in black and white since they had been burned in the past. They did not want difficulties from the school. Besides, my parents had enough on their plates already, so bringing a school problem home was unwelcome. In my entire sixteen-year career in public schools, I brought home good news and nothing more. To respond to these different and separate worlds as a student, I learned early how to keep them apart. School activities were kept not only separate but also incredibly quiet as well. My activities as a member of a large Mexican family living in the United States were kept at home, and nothing from home became part of the school environment. Over time my adaptation to these two environments became a bit smoother. Although my mother was a strong-willed person, physically she was tired from work and responsibility, and her health was not the best. Knowing this well, I kept everything peaceful and to myself. This experience became a great lesson in life, and as a person in the middle of two separate worlds, I became a masterful messenger. I kept the two worlds apart, and my behavior was very different between home and school. There was peace and quietness at school and "normal" life at home.

Like most students, my siblings dropped out of school during the elementary school years. For those few that could move ahead, graduating from junior high school was a big accomplishment that deserved a celebration. So when I joined the Pawnee school, I certainly was looking forward to graduating from junior high. For me at that defining moment, it was a great accomplishment. I remember one of the girls from our neighborhood who made a claim that she would not marry anyone that did not have a junior high education. Those were the standards that we aspired to at that moment in history. Much later, when I was a faculty member at the community college near where I grew up, an Anglo junior high school teacher sought answers for why Mexican American parents make a big deal when their kids graduate from junior high. He said, "When their kids graduate from junior high, they go crazy celebrating." My explanation was based on our background and history as it relates to formal education. So I responded that it was necessary to look at the history of this large group. There were no graduates anywhere. No one in most families had completed eighth grade. Yet despite the mistaken claim that we did not believe in education, we were very proud when someone in the family graduated, no matter what level of the educational system. I am sure that I did not convince him.

I started high school with a high sense of optimism. This was my new opportunity to prove to myself that I could be a good student. Yet I was short of confidence. It is amazing what doubts can do to a person, even to the point of destruction. At home I had no doubts about my abilities. I never questioned them. At school it was a different situation altogether, and I could not find a solution. Although there was a war of contradictions in my brain, I was convinced that I would not retreat but would move forward. Ultimately, these dilemmas turned into opportunities. Going to high school was a turning point in my life. I was heading in a new and different direction where no one in my family before me had gone. As always, I sustained my composure despite doubts about my abilities as a student. These fears and doubts were ultimately overcome, but it certainly took a long time.

What was the status of Mexican American students in school? What was the relationship between school and parents? Looking at the whole scheme of education at the time, if there was an issue at school with Mexican Americans, it was always perceived as the fault of the students or their parents. For example, when Mexican Americans would gradually raise their voices to speak Spanish, the faculty and administrators would respond that this action was against state law. Often the school superintendent was asked to visit us. The superintendent had a soft touch to his delivery. He would start by saying, "Boys and girls, I have been told that you are talking in Spanish on the school grounds, and that is against the state law. It is time for you to change and follow the rules. Don't get me wrong, Spanish is a beautiful language, but people in the community do not speak Castilian, so there is no need to speak it." I believed everything he said! It is unfortunate to claim this, but like many others, I had been conditioned to believe Anglo myths, and there were many. I am convinced that some Anglos felt that they knew more about us than we knew about ourselves. This was one of two attacks that we were getting.

Middle and upper-class Mexicans from Mexico were also critical of the way we spoke Spanish. The inclusion of Tejanos and Tejanas has grown in importance in Texas and elsewhere. For example, in music Tejanos greatly participate and attend the Tejano Music Awards, honoring many Latino/Latina singers, starting with Selena Quintanilla, referred as the Queen of Tejano Music. Political figures like the Castro brothers (Julian and Joaquin) have a national reputation; and in the national media we have known people such as Boris Sanchez and Ana Violeta Navarro, who occupy center stage at CNN and MSNBC, and many others that are nationally and internationally known.

Criticism came from various corners of the community. Language was one of the main issues that remained constant: Our Spanish was faulty, and our accents when we spoke English were discriminated against, especially if it was a "Mexican" accent. One of the reasons I rarely spoke in class was because my accent in English was strong and unacceptable. Now in the world of food, Mexican cuisine has taken national and international recognition. This recognition supersedes Italian and French cuisine, among others. The Catholic religion, a major component of the Mexican tradition and heritage, was also unwelcomed. The philosophy of the public schools was influenced by the Protestant Church. One day while we were in class at Cadillac school, a church leader came to visit us. He spoke to us for a bit, and he proceeded to distribute Bibles to every student at no expense. We did not have any understanding as to the contents of this book, nor did we know the purpose of the distribution. All we knew was that we could not read English. What I was pleased about was that now I owned a book that I never had before. I took it home and showed it to my mother. She did not say anything. That changed when we went to church on Sunday. The Catholic priest was beside himself. The book disappeared at home, and I did not see it again.

English grammar has always been a mystery to me. I used to worry about it a lot. After a long career, I finally stopped worrying about it. I had neither the background for nor an understanding of English grammar. Being unable to comprehend the depth of the subject matter, I relied on memory to pass my courses. I could memorize the hell out of anything. The first English teacher that I had in high school did not help me appreciate the subject matter. Instead of learning grammar, I learned to have great fear of using the grammar since she could easily embarrass you and would criticize you openly in class. Moreover, the study of English grammar was all new to me. It was scary and embarrassing to be sent to the blackboard to do grammatical diagrams when I had difficulty differentiating verbs from nouns and forgot about the more complicated parts of grammar. This experience had a lasting effect on me, even when I was a university professor. Although I kept learning by osmosis in my early years, I never acquired the confidence or the understanding to feel comfortable with how I use the English grammar, but I never stopped writing, and with time my worries left me for good.

Notwithstanding my concerns with English grammar, I was comfortable with the substance of my writing. When I wrote my first book, I asked a person from the English Department to review the manuscript, particularly its grammar. It was against my will and better judgment to show my work to an English professor, mainly because

I was afraid of being laughed at. I was surprised that there were not many grammatical errors, yet I never understood why. This commentary reminds of *Barrio Boy*, a book by Ernesto Galarza, where he discusses how as a second grader in public schools, not knowing English and English grammar were causes for failure and embarrassment.

In my high school years, I was terrified when I had to speak in class. I felt ignorant, and I had a very heavy Spanish accent. It was this part that bothered me the most since I knew that it was not acceptable. I was outright discriminated against, and I was short of strength to handle it. Ms. Moore, the English high school teacher, loved to challenge us and put us on the spot, and that terrified me. In one of her classes, she assigned us each to write a poem and sing it in front of the classroom. I felt that a ton of bricks had fallen on me. Immediately, I felt condemned, like I had been sentenced to die in the electric chair. I came home disillusioned and worrying about what I was going to do. As always, I never wanted my mother to be concerned, so I kept a straight face and pretended that everything was fine, but it was not. I loved to go to school, and I never missed class. By that evening, however, I had not resolved the problem. It was not until the middle of the night that it occurred to me that I was going to call in sick, take an F for the day, and move on. I felt a great sense of guilt in fooling my mother by claiming that I was ill when I was not. I thought that I could live with it since talking before the class was not an option.

By the next morning, I was "sick," and I told mother that I could not go to school because of my illness. Fortunately for me, my mother did not question it, and the day went by without a sweat. By the next morning, I was not "sick" anymore, and I prepared to go back to school with the understanding that Ms. Moore would give me a bad grade for the day, and I would continue to be part of the class. I was incorrect. Ms. Moore was ready for me. The first thing she did was tell that class that I had missed class the prior day, so she was calling me now to recite my poem. I told her that I was not prepared and that I would take a bad grade instead. That was too simple for Ms. Moore. She told me bluntly that I had to do it or else I would fail the class.

Wow! What was I going to do? What would I tell my mother? I always kept things to myself without difficulty, but flunking a course was too much. So I started walking to the front of the classroom, wondering what I was going to do. I was trembling inside and out, but it is amazing what you are able to do when you are under the gun. I started singing to the tune of an old Mexican song and recited a short poem. I do not remember if it rhymed or not, nor how long it was, but the crisis passed, and life went on.

This experience taught me a great lesson in life. Time and again in my personal and professional life, I have been put on the spot, and it is amazing what you can do under difficult circumstances. It makes you a believer in your own talents, and I know now that I can certainly take advantage of this dose of therapeutic confidence.

Our world in South Texas was rooted in the late ninetieth century, fifty years after the American invasion of the Southwest. The considerable increase in immigration from Mexico during and after the Mexican Revolution solidified anti-Mexican attitudes. For all practical purposes, the community was completely ethnically, socially, and culturally divided. Several major Mexican revolts occurred to recapture land in the early twentieth century, but they were unsuccessful. As a result, Mexican Americans were punished and subjugated. The patron system was revitalized by Anglos who came to this area from the South, where some were slave owners.

The level of hostility between the two culturally overlapping groups was not highly visible, yet a constant level of friction was there, and we kept looking at each other in a world of silence that was still, at times, somewhat explosive. Neil Foley documents this history in *The White Scourge*. In this book Foley challenges our understanding of race in the United States and disentangles the complexity of the history of ethnicity in the cotton culture in Texas. Other sources give an account of this tragic era in the Southwest, which was far more pronounced and odious in South Texas. Compounding this social situation were the traditional attitudes of class-oriented Mexicans toward Tejanos. The Mexican upper class had a long history of subduing the lower classes. As wealthy Mexicans moved back to Mexico after the American invasion of the Southwest, the Anglos were natural replacements for the Mexican elites. Time and again, when we visited some of our folks in Monterrey, Nuevo León, social discrimination was rampant. It started with the use of the Spanish language. To this day, a lot of the old Tejanos apologize for their inability to speak "proper" Spanish. It took me years to realize that our Spanish was sound and communicative and that an apology was unnecessary since this kind of discrimination was based on ignorance and prejudice. How could we have spoken "proper" Spanish when at the time it was prohibited in the school system, and there was no formal or informal education to accomplish this goal? To begin with, what is "proper Spanish"? Heaven knows, I guess!

When I graduated from high school at the ripe age of 22, the military was ready to draft me soon after graduation, The preparation and examination to become part of the military started at Fort Sam Houston, San Antonio. Mentally, I prepared to pass the examination. When I was growing up during World War II, I saw countless Tejanos making the same trip to San Antonio to take the physical exam, and most of them would not pass it. My brother José Gonzalo and Alfredo Garcia, a neighbor, were the only ones in the entire community to pass the exam. For whatever reason, it never occurred to us why they did not pass the exam. We generally assumed that if a candidate took the physical and did not pass, they were *enfermos* (physically sick). Yet after the examination, they continued to work, and for the most part they were good workers, good hunters, and excellent sharpshooters. Surely the military lost a great opportunity by failing to attract these potential recruits. Much later it became clear to me that the failure to make the cut had nothing to do with illness or ability. It mainly had to do with language issues. Most of them did not know how to read or write in English. Obviously, they would fail the written exam, and the military did not make exceptions. My brother and Alfredo knew enough English to pass the exam.

That being said, when I joined the other recruits to make that special drive to San Antonio in the summer of 1958, I was determined to pass the examination, not because I wanted to join the military but because I wanted to prove that the issue was not about failing the physical but about a language barrier. I wanted to enroll immediately and serve the two-year requirement. My mother was not convinced that this was the best strategy. She had one son who went to war, and she wanted to avoid repeating the experience if possible. I did not disagree with her, but I felt that I did not have another alternative. Why wait? There was a vague possibility that I could go to college, but there was nothing that I could see on the horizon.

Pawnee High characterized the rural environment of South Texas. Small, isolated, economically poor, and nothing on the horizon to attract young people to stay, particularly Anglo youth. The high school student population was about fifty-six, and my class was composed of a total of sixteen students. Approximately 60 percent of the student body was Latinos at that time. The percentage was far higher in the lower grades. As noted previously, most of the Anglo students would leave the area as soon as they graduated from high school, although many of their parents owned sizeable amounts of farmland. However, for *la raza* families with fewer opportunities and less education for jobs—and with closer, tighter, larger, more homogenous family ties—there was no place to go but to stay home and work at the farm. Even to this day, some of the Latinos who grew up around Pawnee still live there. Most have jobs in the surrounding towns, but Pawnee is home. The Anglos, with very few exceptions, left the community for good, either to go to universities or to more lucrative jobs elsewhere in urban areas. Unquestionably, they were far more mobile and integrated than we were. We see each other only at school reunions. Once I interviewed an old Anglo woman who had live in Pawnee since she was little. She told me that when she was young, there was only one Mexican American family (the Laras), but now she is the only Anglo in Pawnee.

It never occurred to me that soon I would leave the community for good. At this point in time, I could not see further than finishing high school, since that was my goal. I felt that graduating from high school would be a major triumph for my family, and it was. I thought I had plenty on my plate, and I was going to make it work. Sadly, college was not on my radar. Yet this became a pattern in my professional career. I normally never projected far into the future. Instead, I concentrated on the work before me. Yet this concentration on hard work opened the way for new adventures. When this happened, I would craft every step carefully. These were small steps, but they were many, and I was never disappointed. These careful steps gradually took a long way. In a matter of a few short years, I became a professor at a community college.

Let me divert for a moment of this story to address an important occasion that relates to my high school. In my second year at Bee County College, I was invited to be the commencement speaker of the graduating class of 1968 at Pawnee High School. The request came from the graduating students through the superintendent. What a contrast of events in a matter of ten years since graduating in 1958. I felt humbled and honored, and it was a personal triumph. I was going back to a place where I had started to dream of possible success despite discrimination, humiliation, and deep habits of being subordinate and, for the most part, a nonperson. Moreover, one of the senior graduates was my nephew and *ahijado* (godchild), Carlos Chapa.

So one evening my wife, kids, and I came to Pawnee to make the presentation. One of my college colleagues also made the trip to experience the event. I wondered what kind of introduction I was going to get from Pete Marecek, the superintendent. As I walked to the stage for the ceremony in the small high school auditorium, the same auditorium that we used to assemble in, where the same superintendent would warn us not to speak Spanish, I was truly mesmerized. As I looked up to see the crowd, I knew just about everybody—such a pleasure, yet I was nervous and scared. I noticed that the Latino attendance was high. Part of the reason for the greater number of

Mexican Americans was that I was the first Latino ever invited to give the commencement address in this small community. By the way, I was the last person of Mexican decent to speak in this ceremony. As the ceremony got underway, the superintendent got up and welcomed the parents and relatives of the students who were about to graduate. He told the audience that this was a special occasion. He then proceeded to introduce the commencement speaker—me. Once again, I wondered what he was going to say. Well, this is exactly what he said: "Ladies and Gentlemen, our commencement speaker tonight is Dr. Villarreal." He moved back to his seat, and I asked myself, "Is that it?" It was not that I wanted him to say more, I was just surprised. At that point I took off with my presentation. I was so prepared that I memorized practically every word I said. Today, I don't remember a word. All I knew was that I was breaking the barriers, and that was critical to me. I did not even have a doctoral degree at the time—it was still seven years away. But Pete told me later that he knew I was going to get it so he might as well get used to it and refer to me as "Dr." before anyone else.

There is a moral to this story: For years Pete Marecek contemplated getting a doctoral degree in administration, and he never did it. He was paying his respects to a person who he never dreamed could achieve the same goal. He told me many times that I was one of the most persistent and tenacious people that he had ever known. I am convinced that Marecek was happy that a Hispanic from his school was going to get a doctoral degree—the first and the last.

In the spring of my senior year at Texas A&I University, I had a call from Pete Marecek asking me if I wanted to teach in Pawnee. I hesitated since I was looking for a position at a high school somewhere in Texas. Although I needed a job badly, I had other, more altruistic motives that I wanted to pursue. One of the leading motives was to try to break the barriers historically organized by Anglos to reduce the participation of people of Mexican origin in mainstream America. Although this presented a difficult task—and it was, indeed, a solo act—I felt compelled in the name of my parents to explore this alternative. So coming to Pawnee to teach migrants at the elementary level was not challenging enough. Moreover, teaching migrants would put me in a subordinate position, just as it did before. With this intent I proceed to write application letters to high schools across the state of Texas. I sent 207 letters to 207 school districts. All the work of typing 207 letters on an old typewriter produced only two responses, and they were negative. Not having one single other option, I took the position in Pawnee. It only took one semester of teaching to realize that I needed to further my formal education. In the spring semester of 1963, I started working on a master's degree in science. John Joshlin, my middle school principal, and I traveled two hundred miles every Saturday to take six semester hours at Texas A&I University. I was ready for new avenues and adventures, and one possibility was to further my formal education.

The journey of teaching elementary school lasted for nine months. I resigned at the end of the school year. My plan was to teach secondary education in Pawnee, but that became impossible. The coach who was teaching social sciences was fired at midsemester, and I applied for his position, but I never had a response. Finally, at the end of the school year, I went to see the superintendent. Pete Marecek was frank with me. He told me that the school board was not ready to hire a Mexican American to teach high school students. He told me that it would take ten to twenty years before they would allow a person of Mexican origin to teach at the high school. This ended my dreams and hopes of teaching there and was the cause for me to resign.

I was hired to teach migrant students and migrant students only. Although I had a university degree, unlike some of the established faculty members, it was unacceptable for me to teach Anglos. Although I knew this well, I was trying to break social, ethnic, and cultural barriers. This and other experiences had an enormous and lasting impact on me as I navigated the world of education. Knowing these circumstances, I continued my graduate studies that summer, wondering what was coming next: a new job teaching secondary students or the military.

Conceivably, this was not a rational decision, but it certainly was based on principle. My actions left me without a job, and the military was waiting. Out of these experiences, I had only one regret: leaving my family to go elsewhere, particularly my mother, who, I am certain, was in great pain that one of her immediate family members was leaving for good. And she was right; I never came back home to stay again. Yet I am grateful that I could spend a good year with my parents, brothers, sisters, uncles, aunts, other relatives, and friends. Regretfully, that would never happen again. While a graduate student at Texas A&I University, I continued to pursue new avenues for jobs. Days before school started, I was hired as a biology teacher at Pharr–San Juan–Alamo High School, the very center of the Rio Grande Valley.

When I was hired by the school district, my understanding was that I was going to teach biology at the high school. But in a matter of two days, it became questionable about teaching in high school. I was notified that there was a problem and that problem meant I would not be allowed to teach biology in high school. I was told that I had a heavy Spanish accent and the administration was sensitive to "Mexican" accents. My academic credentials were not questioned. I was qualified to teach biology, but I was too Mexican for them. So after a day or two of debate among the administrators, I was brought by the high school principal before the superintendent of the tri-city school district. Now I was in a situation where an ignorant and prejudiced administrator was going to determine how much of an accent I had and what needed to be done to correct it. After a brief interview, the superintendent told me that I had a bad accent, and he gave me six weeks to change it. As we know, accents are not removed overnight. Anyway, I was allowed to teach biology, and after six weeks, the principal took me back to the superintendent for a second interview. He told me that I had improved and that I should come back again in another six weeks. I guess that they gave up on me, because I was never asked to come back again. I knew what the deal was: The timing was on my side since classes were starting, and they had no one to teach biology.

It worked. I was never questioned again. Three years later, I voluntarily left the position to become a doctoral student. Ironically, one year later I met Townley, the superintendent, on the campus at the University of Texas at Austin. At that time, both of us were doctoral students. The meeting was short since he failed to recognize me. I never saw him again. The following year I transferred to the University of Oklahoma.

Socially, moving to the lower Rio Grande Valley was a new experience that I never had before. It was a culture shock, and teaching in a large school district was challenging. For the most part, I was well accepted by the faculty, administration, and students. When I became an authority figure in the classroom, some students were uncomfortable. With good intent and over time, life at school became easier. On the other hand, my social life expanded considerably from my early years. Now it was time to grow. This changed rapidly, and I learned that I had talents I had never known before. I guess I was becoming a real Escamilla, and according to my wife, they were real lovers. Life was joyous, and in my third year at this border community, I married Norma. Meanwhile, I continued to drive to Kingsville on Saturdays in hopes that I would finish my master's degree.

In chapter 5 I continue to discuss and analyze different variations of overcoming struggles and discovering newer avenues, a source of strength. Yet in my pursuit for a better world, academy and family continued to be separate. My hope was that, ultimately, I would narrow the gap between these two important institutions.

Chapter 5

Trying to Reach the Sky Without Direction

There were three pending issues when we returned from the senior trip to Mexico: the Army was waiting for me; I kept thinking that I would find a path to attend college; and the immediate concern of working long hours in the field, either pulling broomcorn or picking cotton.

Part of my curriculum at Pawnee High was agricultural courses. For the most part, I enjoyed the classes, and I participated in several grass and dairy judging contests. With a streak of winning contents, we ended at Texas A&M University, a place that I did not know existed. Louis Turner was the perennial agriculture teacher. One afternoon as I was walking out of the classroom, he called me to tell me that he had a brother at A&I University in Kingsville who was dean of students, and he was planning to see him over the summer. He asked me if I wanted to go with him. I immediately took the opportunity. I knew this was my chance to visit a university. But the summer came and Turner never called. As the days went by, I lost faith that I would be going to meet him. My saviors were Poncho Serna, a neighbor, and my brother José Gonzalo.

Friday night dances were extremely popular in Nell, Texas, during the summer. This is a small community out in the boonies, about seven miles from where I grew up. During the hot and humid summer months, we toiled long hours, pulling broomcorn, picking cotton, or picking corn. Since social gatherings were uncommon in our community, we looked forward to these events. Typically, weather permitting, a large crowd would gather at Nell to participate in the Samoras' rectangular concrete platform for dancing where all the social action took place. Polo, who ran the Friday night dance, was an employee of the owner of the general store and cantina. Polo would invite *conjuntos* (South Texas musical group style) to perform. Of course, there was bingo and everything else that made for good local entertainment. This was the biggest social gathering in the community. This was a great place for boys to meet girls and girls to meet boys. Among the many attendees were the Serna family, our neighbors and friends who lived just a half mile from us. My parents were good compadres of Aurelio and Luisa Serna. Both Aurelio and Luisa were also compadres of mine. I grew up with most of their kids, and we went to Cadillac and Lentz Elementary Schools together. Poncho was the oldest of the family. A handsome young man, he was a very personable, nice, quiet, decent, warm, and amiable human being. Everyone got along with Poncho since he was kindhearted and gentle.

One Friday evening at the dance, Poncho and I engaged in a conversation, and I told him that I wanted to go to A&I University but that Turner had never appeared. Poncho reminded me that he had family near Kingsville in the small community of Riviera, and he was willing to drive me there and drop me off for the day while he visited his family. I thought that it was a great idea. The problem was that neither he nor I had access to an automobile. I thought about it, and I decided to ask my older brother if he could lend me his car for one day. As always, my brother was most cooperative and happy to be of help.

To Kingsville we went in early August. Poncho dropped me off, and I went searching for something that would get me admitted. I was clueless about the whole process. I did not know that you had to apply, qualify, and register. All I knew was that I had graduated with a B+ average from Pawnee High, and I wanted to attend college full-time. Otherwise, I looked like a lowly farm hand; I spoke English with a heavy Spanish accent, I was very shy, my hands were covered with warts, and I was ignorant about the world, particularly the university. I had a few things going for myself: I had the right attitude, I worked hard, I was focused, and I was an ambitious student. I wanted to make it at all costs. At this juncture my goal was for my mother and father to be proud that one of their kids was attending a university. This accomplishment (to attend college) probably was not significant to someone else, but to me it was the ultimate reward to my parents.

I don't remember what I did to register, but I did. At this point in time, my goal was to attend the university for six weeks until they discovered that I was not college material and dropped me for good. Once home, I would tell folks that I had gone to college. But that changed and the university became part of my life. It raised my spirits forever. I entered the university with low expectations of myself but with great ambition to succeed. I chose elementary education as a major. Why? Simply because elementary education appeared the easiest way to make the grade, and I wanted to pass at least some of the courses. The ideal me had far bigger plans on the horizon, but I was too intimidated, and the best that I could do was to be an elementary teacher. I thought that I needed time to resolve several issues. Mind you, teaching elementary school is most important, but in my case, I was looking for bigger things and not knowing what they were.

The good folks at the university apparently understood my plight, and in no time, I became part of the 635-member freshman class of fall 1958. The first gathering of the freshmen was in an auditorium to provide an introduction and give the parameters of being a good student. The speaker at this meeting gave us an immediate warning that if we were able to succeed, we had to work hard. Moreover, he claimed that approximately 225 members of the class would graduate in the next four years. He continued by telling us that there were many reasons why students dropped out. The statistics stressed that two-thirds of this freshman group would not make it to the end of the four-year program. This statement hit me like a ton of bricks. I looked around, and practically everyone looked brighter and smarter than I. Most of the students there were Anglos, and I associated Anglos with being brighter and smarter than Mexicans. Later I realized that I correlated brightness with whiteness, with no evidence that it was true. How was I going to overcome this rugged mountain before me? Well, I had already crossed several mountains, why not this one? Still, it was easier said than done. Four years later, more than two hundred students were part of my graduating class. I was graduating legitimately, without honors, but it did not matter. I had earned a B average, and I was proud of my accomplishments. I had obtained a bachelor's degree, the first in the entire history of my large family that had lived in this area for generations.

I came home from that first visit to Kingsville with great news, and my mother, among others, shared those sentiments. I immediately told her that there was money involved for tuition and books, as well as a place to stay. Mama told me that she would work with Dad on this. Knowing Antonia Escamilla Villarreal, I had full confidence that she would find the money, although I knew that, as always, we were very short of funds.

When I registered at the university, I noticed the kind of clothes the students were generally wearing, and I really wanted to conform to those standards. Accordingly, I told my mother that I needed to buy some clothes and shoes. Mother took care of those needs.

After I registered for the fall semester in 1958, I went to the local military board to inform them that I was going to be a full-time student and that I wanted an extension since the Army was ready to take me. I visited the local board in Karnes City, and I was given permission to attend the university. Unfortunately, the commitment was not in writing. I proceeded to attend during the fall semester thinking that everything was settled. I soon learned that verbal agreements do not count.

Sunday afternoon came, and my extended family and friends gathered to wish me well and send me off. My Uncle Gregorio, my mother's younger brother, and my double cousins, Gollo, Chindo, Miro, and Beto, showed up for the occasion. My thoughts were on how I was ever going to make it in college. I did not want to disappoint my parents, yet I was convinced that my stay at the university was going to be short. Much later, I learned that students could attend a university for years without graduating or being sent back home. Despite my fear and ignorance, I took the chance, and it worked. My calculated six-week stay at the university turned into undergraduate and graduate studies and more than sixty years of professional life at colleges and universities. I had the honor to teach at all levels of the educational system, from elementary to graduate students; I became a researcher; and I was involved in different levels of administrative positions.

The first semester at A&I was exciting and challenging. I stayed in the men's dormitory the first semester. The change of lifestyle and circumstances was dramatic. I was moving from a rural, lower-class environment to a middle-class environment composed of mostly Anglos from all over the state and the nation. Now I had running water, a bathroom, a roommate, and a variety of regulations set by the university. There were no more parents, siblings, uncles, or aunts, nor field labor to complete, at least during the week. My long years of isolation were coming to an end. I felt good. I sensed that I was getting somewhere and I had made the right decision. I questioned my ability to compete, but I was ready to try. It was the beginning of many changes to come, but the most important part was to be a full-time student; I was studying hard, and I was passing the courses that I was taking.

Struggling with assimilation and acculturation continued to be part of my journey, although it was getting better. Another part of the struggle was the poor preparation I had received in high school.

The gap between high school and university was considerable, but the biggest struggle was with myself. In the long run, all these battles served me well. In no time at all, I became part of a set of middle-class values that I had never experienced before. I took the challenge with enthusiasm and moved forward.

I was convinced that these changes would result in me becoming more accepted in the adopted environment. The challenge to change as soon as it is necessary has remained with me for my entire life. Yet it seems that the more we change, the more we remain the same. I see it in myself. Like many people, I have gone through major changes in life, but often it seems that I remain the same the way I was raised. But there is difference. I grew up shy and, in public, not sociable. I was afraid. Now, I am amazingly comfortable in any kind of setting. I can easily change according to the circumstances. This was not true when I was a kid. I enjoy and feel comfortable moving from one end of the spectrum to the other with ease and understanding. Although during adulthood I lived in a different world, I never alienated my family. I am very much part of where I started during my childhood.

In my first years in higher education, I found myself somewhat overcome by the magnitude of the university. The grandiosity of the place was phenomenal, exciting, and challenging. It was a place to grow. In my whole life, nothing has intrigued me more than the challenge and struggle of growing up. Although I am in the winter of my years, I am still as excited about growing through learning as I was when I was a high school student. Every day is a groundbreaking adventure, and each new set of ideas becomes part of me. I see the world with so many possibilities of work that needs to be done.

In the fall of 1958, A&I University was barely beginning to feel the impact of Latino students. The purported position of the university at that time was to treat all students equally, though they were mostly unequal. Universities, like other educational entities, reflect the culture of communities and regions. The question of ethnic oppression, racism, and inequality were very much in existence. Historically, universities were not established for minorities. A&I University reflected the problems and animosity found in the community and across Texas.

When I registered for classes in my sophomore year, I was short one class, so I saw a course in Spanish and tried to register. I could not take it because I had not taken the prerequisite Spanish courses in high school. There were no Spanish classes taught at Pawnee High, nor could we use the Spanish language on the school grounds. That being the case, I went to see the chair of the department. He was a Spaniard who knew little about the community, particularly the dilemma of Mexican Americans. Not having the experience of taking high school classes in Spanish was the best motive not to be admitted. I could, however, take a Spanish course for nonspeakers. I took the course with a group of Anglos, and after a week I decided to drop it since it was too elementary. This and other policies were established to cater to the Anglos. There was no opportunity to take a standardized exam to replace the prerequisite.

The university did not depend on minorities as they do now, and as a result, some of the policies have been modified or changed. So what is wrong with being treated equally? The issue here is that the equality was superficial; the policies of the university had been designed for one group with one set of values. Some of us who became political activists knew the difference, but back then we did not have the support, the skills, or the necessary connections. The other side did not see the problems. Nothing was broken, so there was no need to fix it.

Social life at A&I was limited since I spent considerable time studying to catch up. I became known as the "monk" in our dormitory. Being in South Texas, A&I reflected the social, historical, and cultural environment of the dominant community. At that time it was rare for a Latino to date an Anglo woman. On the other hand, it was not uncommon for a male Anglo to date a Latina. There were not a lot of Latinas attending the university anyway. So we Tejanos ended up on the short end of the stick for sure.

I have spent my entire life challenging the inequities of the system. So it shouldn't be surprising that I started dating an Anglo woman that I met in class. She was not from the area, and that made a difference. She was from the Houston area, and though I did not date her for a long time, it was a short step toward greater integration. At that time the social environment called for Mexican Americans with Mexican Americans and Anglos with Anglos. My first semester at A&I, I lived in university dorms, which were composed mostly of Anglos. By the end of my first semester, I had concluded that financially, I could not afford to continue to live there, as much as I wanted to stay. I moved to an apartment about three blocks from the university. All student members in these apartments were male Mexican Americans. I remained there until I graduated from the university.

Considering all the obstacles that I faced daily, I was making a rapid transition, embracing the institution and the community in a university system that was moving at a snail's pace. At this stage of development, the policies of the university had neither sensitivity to nor an understanding of the dilemma of minorities. If there was an issue on this score, I took the blame, and I was able to survive under critical conditions. For those of us who were able to make the transition from one political culture to another, we made no demands, we made no excuses, and the transition was made in painful silence. It was the way of life, and we dared not challenge the system until later. Much later in my career as an academician, I joined a more mature university, and I fully realized the inadequacies of the educational system in higher education and its treatment of minorities. By this time I had learned to join groups with similar goals and fight.

By the time I graduated in 1962 with a bachelor's degree in biology and history, the Civil Rights Movement was beginning to show its face among the Chicano youth in South Texas. But not even at the height of the Civil Rights Movement was there any support from the Anglo community. It was a Chicano thing. For a long time, Mexican Americans were ingrained in the past, to the detriment of their own good. Nevertheless, older Mexican Americans condemned the labyrinth of the Anglo community. They were angry and frustrated since they were denied their right to liberty and justice. To the contrary, there was a strong sense of admiration for Anglos and what they stood for. This respect and fear paralleled a strong sense of being naturally subordinate. Perhaps in some ways some of us wanted to be Anglos. Yet I remained proud of our rich heritage and what we had accomplished.

In my early years at the university, I was convinced that if I had any chance to make it, I had to be a serious student, particularly when I questioned my intelligence. Regrettably, I had been persuaded to feel lesser than the Anglos. This proved to be costly in dealing with academic work. I knew the problem, but I could not get rid of it. To fight this dilemma, I turned to books and studied hard. I did not go out anywhere, not even to the dining area of the student union building. It was all classes, studying, and working at the farm over the weekends. I studied long hours, trying to narrow the gap between high school and university work. I had a sense of optimism that I was going to make it regardless. I was, perhaps, too idealistic, but it made me feel good from time to time.

Although I had learned in high school to study hard, I began to question the methodology that I was following to get where I wanted. There was a downside to this strength: I was not being myself. I continued to be subordinate, and there was a sense of isolation in all my activities. By Friday of every week, I was ready to go home to help Dad out in the field. I worked the entire weekend, then I would get ready to go back to the university, and my mother and sisters would pack me food and clothes for the week.

By mid-October, just before my birthday, I got a notification from the Army telling me to report to the military base in San Antonio. I was shocked since I had asked for permission from the recruitment office in Karnes City. But as I said before, the permission was not done in writing. I immediately took the letter to the academic dean, seeking support to solve the problem. Dean Jernigan, who later became president of the institution, took a hard look at me, and said, "How did you manage to get in this mess?" He asked me some questions and then he called the recruitment office in Karnes City. He asked if I could obtain permission to continue my studies at the university. The local board officer agreed to the request on the condition that he needed a written letter making the request by the end of that day. I went to my apartment, drafted a letter, then drove more than 112 miles before the five-o'clock deadline. Permission was granted. The incident was most significant to me. Without permission I would have gone to the military and probably never would have acquired formal education. Personally, I did not mind being drafted to join the Army. But being educated was everything to me.

English was my worst subject, chiefly grammar. It was not a question of not trying, because I did. My first English class at the university was taught by Ms. Gantz. She was pretentious, very tight and protective of herself, and she was convinced of the superiority of the English language. Ms. Gantz joined many professors on campus who had little or no understanding of other cultures, even though they were born and raised in South Texas. Minorities at that time were taken for granted. The perception was that what we needed to do was to join the majority, and our problems would be resolved. Everybody was treated according to the same standards, and no efforts were made to bend down and pull us up. I understood well that I was not prepared, but I was willing to make a difference if given the opportunity. With Ms. Gantz I worked hard, but I could not pass a single exam. I never forgot when she gave us research assignments for the semester. She brought to class an English-style bowler hat, and inside the hat she had all the titles for the assigned research papers neatly folded. Everything was done cautiously and with great neatness and precision. I drew mine and read it carefully. My research assignment was titled "Nonverbal Highway Signs in Latin America." I searched the library for six weeks and found nothing on the subject. I came to see her with a request to change the title since I had no adequate information to complete the assignment. She looked at me and directly told me she would not change it and for me to go back and complete my assignment. Another two weeks went by and nada. I went to see her again to ask for a change, but no dice. At that point I took control of what I was doing, and I changed the title. The new title was "The Pan American Highway," with all the pageantry and color of this historical road. I got a solid F. This was too much for an unprepared freshman.

When the final examination came, I took it seriously and worked the entire period allowed in hopes that it would make a difference. I received an F, the only F in my entire university career. In July 1975, when I finished my dissertation and obtained a doctoral degree in political science from University of Oklahoma, I did something very unusual. I do not know if I am proud of it or not. I sent to Ms. Gantz a copy of my 358-page dissertation, and I asked her to please correct the grammar. I never got an answer, nor did I ever expect one.

Except for the class in English grammar, the rest of the classes went well. I was not making high marks since I was busy bridging the knowledge gap. However, I was learning, and I was learning fast. For the most part, I enjoyed the classes and being a university student. I was beginning to see the light at the end of the tunnel, and I began to feel important. Little by little I was becoming one of them. Still, I worked my tail off. I was perceived as a monk, staying in my room for long hours. I only stepped out to go to classes and eat. The first semester I stayed in the men's dorm. Despite my social inactivity I truly enjoyed the dorm. It was so different: I had running water with a commode, the room was air conditioned with a nice window, and the food in the cafeteria was wonderful—not that it wasn't at home. What else could I want except to study and study hard?

Living in the dormitory was a most satisfying experience. The change of environment was so drastic that I took full advantage. Across the hall there were two Houston seniors majoring in engineering who wondered why I was such a hermit. One day they came and knocked at the door and invited me to go with them to have a cup of coffee. I think that I showed shyness, humility, and, perhaps, embarrassment as we walked to the student union. But I was so proud and felt so privileged to be in this circle. I kept thinking and dreaming, wondering when I would pull out of my shell and become free by being myself. I knew that when I did this, I would do far better. I would certainly enjoy life more, and, more important to me, I would become a leader and the "big man on campus." Yet the short and simple experience of walking with two students that I knew little but cared a lot about had a lasting impact on me. I will never forget their faces or the brief conversation that we had.

Anglo and Tejano students were socially divided on campus, just like everywhere else. Predictably, Anglos had the upper hand. But there was a major exception. Huge number of students were coming from Laredo to A&I. Their presence and culture made a world of difference. Living in Laredo made these students very "Mexican," and its culture was most accepting to me. Every year while I was there as a student, the Laredo students would vote for their preferred person as the Annual Queen of the Year. They always had enough votes. The Laredo crowd was practically all Latinos. This was all new to me. At that point in my life, I had never seen Hispanics having a majority vote for a queen. I was surprised and happy. The students from Laredo were in a less discriminatory environment. Interestingly, however, when Friday afternoon came, most of them would drive home every week. They were in love with Laredo. In one of the apartments that I stayed in off campus, all the residents were from Laredo. The building was empty every weekend. Unquestionably, the way they saw the relations between us and the Anglos had a huge impact on me. I learned from them to better stand up to our surroundings.

Unlike the roommates that I had off campus from Laredo, the roommate that I had at the university dorm was an unusual person. Rudy was a literary giant who was majoring in English literature. Fundamentally, he was a nice human being, but he was emotionally juvenile, strange, eccentric, and spoiled. He was the only child of a middle-class family from the city of Falfurrias. Not only was he spoiled, but he also had no common sense. He had difficulty knowing what he wanted out of life. Staying in the dorm included access to a wonderful cafeteria that I took full advantage. Rudy never did. He would go out to eat fast food even though he was already paying for the meals in the cafeteria. On several occasions his father would come to visit, providing moral and financial support and consoling him. During his father's visits, I would dismiss myself so they could have an open conversation. In the process I was learning a lot. Rudy served a good purpose. He was an intellectual. My intuition for the intellectual part of life was nourished by Rudy's presence.

When I started university, one of my high school classmates also attended the same university. My father lent me his car to travel to school. My classmate, Lance, did not have a car, so he would ride with me on a weekly basis. In my search for equality, this was the first time in my life that I had the opportunity to be on equal basis with an Anglo. In high school we had known each other well, but the relationship was different. Lance came from a prominent Anglo family in the community. More than prominence was that he was an Anglo and the salutatorian of my high school graduation class. As the year progressed, I gained ground, and we became equals. I look at it now and am able to wonder what the big deal was. At that given moment, though, it meant a lot to me. I wanted badly to be among equals. Much later in life, I visited with Lance at a high school reunion, and I even had more status than he did. Lance became one of my admirers.

By the end of the spring semester at the university, my grades were decent, and my confidence had improved. There were still rough edges from my rural background that I was modifying. Life was beginning to be better, and I could see that I was going to hang around for a while. I was a full-time student taking fifteen hours per semester, and by the end of the spring I had accumulated twenty-nine semester hours, one semester hour short of being a sophomore. That bothered me greatly. How could I tell my folks that I had not passed to the next grade? How could I tell my friends and classmates that I was a sophomore when I was not? Looking back, I am certain that most people did not care one way or another. What counted was that I had twenty-nine semester hours and not whether I was a sophomore or not.

But life was radically different at home, and grades and passing were not critical issues. I think that my family assumed that I would do all right, and, besides, it was my work and my business. I don't remember my mother, father, or siblings ever asking me if I had passed or not. It was a nonissue. I took it in stride and never told anyone. My mother focused on family matters and for something far deeper and more basic than me being a freshman or a sophomore at a university. Besides, she had confidence in me to handle school properly, and I greatly appreciated that. The summer of 1959 arrived, and I was fully immersed in toiling in the fields. Higher education was on hold until the fall semester. As an undergraduate, I never went to summer school until the summer before my senior year. Since I decided to double major (history and biology), it took a bit longer to finish. I went for six weeks during my senior year so I could finish in exactly four years.

As far as I could tell, nothing had changed at home. Life went on the same as it had in years past. The preoccupation with survival and harvesting the crops was ultimate, and Dad set the pace for all of us to follow. I had learned that if I put in a good summer of work, there would be a way for me to go back to school to finish my degree. The same could be said about my friends and other relatives. Life went on as usual. If education was discussed, it was in social terms. Anglos in our community kept a watchful eye on my educational efforts, often with curiosity and sometimes with disdain. A few went to the extent of letting me know that my place was to be a farm worker. I was violating the rules of the community. Call it a mindset of historic proportions.

Throughout the four years of my bachelor's degree, I worked at the farm with my brothers, sisters, and countless workers Dad hired to harvest the crops on time. We would work long and hard for five to six days a week, from sunup to sundown. Saturday afternoons were a time to go to Kenedy to socialize, buy groceries, and do whatever other activities we needed to do. Since there was no tradition for my family or for most Mexican Americas to attend school, education was not part of the picture. During these college years I kept an eye on clothes and shoes for the coming semesters. In Kenedy, like most small South Texas communities, the clothing stores had decent clothing and shoes. The first suit that I bought was in Kenedy. I bought it in the first year that I was teaching in Pawnee. The school required me to take a picture once a year, so I bought a black suit. When Norma became my girlfriend, I gave her that picture. Today, the picture is on her nightstand beside her bed. The picture has been part of her for more than sixty years.

We always looked forward to visiting Kenedy since it was an opportunity for boys and girls to meet. At that time these small communities were prosperous and active. Changes in the economy in recent years have dealt a brutal blow to small communities in South Texas and throughout the country, and Kenedy is a prime example of this phenomenon. Like everywhere else, chain stores like Wal-Mart and HEB have taken center stage, and locally owned stores have almost disappeared. For those of us who are older and saw this transition, we continue to be nostalgic.

By the time I was attending the university, four of my siblings had married, and they had their own homes and children. My sisters Oralia and Minerva lived with my parents. There was another addition to the family who had joined us when I was 10 years old. This was Hilario, one of the two of the twins (the other was Maria Elena), children of my sister Hortensia. When my sister gave birth, she was unable to recuperate well and she needed help. My sister Oralia went to live with them in Premont, Texas, while she would take care of Hortensia and the twins. As things continued, it was decided one of the twins would stay with Dad and Mom. Instead of staying temporarily as was planned, Hilario stayed with us until he got married in 1971. My parents had a firm and unwritten policy that when one of their children married, they had to move out of the house for good. As my father used to say, *es harina de otro costal* (it is flour from another bag).

The last two years that I spent in pursuit of a bachelor's degree, I worked part of the summer at the local Pawnee cotton gin. I was the only Latino among the workers. Formally, I was the most educated person in the group. Yet I was given the hardest job. I would run the sucker, the giant tube that sucks the cotton to the gin. I was working a few hundred feet from where I had attended school. Throughout this summer work, I felt that good days were ahead for me. I was succeeding at the university, things were good at home, and I felt far better about myself. In the community, I was the only Hispanic attending a university. The Anglos were well aware of what was happening, but the issue was never discussed. It was simply not happening. Things changed, however, and by the time I acquired my first university degree, a couple of neighbors who worked together with me at the gin felt lesser. They told me that I was looking down on them. I didn't think I was, but I knew that things were changing in the community. This was not good for some Anglos.

As the summers continued in my first four years of education, the social and familial environment at home continued unchanged. Life went on as it had prior to my attending high school and university. The family was fully aware that for the first time a member of the family was getting an education, and they did not question my performance or anything else as far as my activities at the university went. My response was similar. I never used my educational status in any way against my family or anyone else. It was not me. I had strong reminders of my Uncle Santiago. His social behavior of demeaning the social qualities of family members was a characteristic well-known to us. Fortunately, I did not suffer from those social anxieties. I kept pace with the family without disturbing the peace and serenity of family life. From the university perspective, however, it was quite different. My world was roiling and in constant change. The challenges of the academic world were changing my outlook on life, including my social, cultural, and political values. I was becoming politicized, and had all the characteristics of a liberal idealist. It was not difficult for me to tell that every summer I went to work out in the field I was looking at the world with different eyes.

In my early childhood, I enjoyed stories about the history of Mexico and the United States. I knew more about Mexican history because I was surrounded by Mexicans, and during my early years, the memories of the Mexican Revolution was still in full furor in South Texas. Don Abundio, the blind man who taught me how to read in Spanish, had many stories about the revolution. He was the product of this tragic decade (1910–1920). When I was asked to declare my major, I said that I was an elementary education major, but as soon as I had the opportunity, I changed it to history, not knowing that in the long run I would not be able to get a job. So in college I took a lot of courses in history. In the process of taking history courses, I took a class with a professor named Dr. Coleson. I fell in love with how he saw and interpreted history. Dr. Coleson was a Texas native who had grown up in Uvalde. For the first time in my life, a history teacher recognized the importance of Mexican American history. The university did not offer courses in Mexican history, but Dr. Coleson would include regional history and had a strong handle on the flavor of our culture. A University of Oklahoma graduate, his dissertation was on Mexican immigration. His classes were flooded with Mexican American students. In this situation, my love for history increased. I took his courses as an undergraduate as well as a graduate student. After I completed all the required courses, he directed my thesis.

History and politics go hand in hand. In time I became fascinated with politics, particularly power politics. I found this intriguing since power greatly influences human behavior. I acquired a great appreciation for the study of human behavior. Politics is a hard subject. The study of politics is a study of conflict between individuals, groups, and nations. During my early years in college, I had no understanding of the political system. But as I continued my studies, I connected politics with justice and equality, subjects familiar to me. From there I thought I could teach politics not only to Mexican Americans but also to Anglos. My hope was that I would be able to teach them about our American political system. This would provide great legitimacy for me, and it certainly has. All along I kept thinking about how I was going to come up to par with the Anglos. What better way than to teach Anglos the American political system! That is what I have done for more than sixty years at all levels of the educational system, from elementary to doctoral students.

In a matter of less than four years while attending the university in hopes to acquire a bachelor's degree, I was able to acquire a masterful balance between these two dominant cultures. Unquestionably, it has been a great benefit to know two languages that are used worldwide. On a two-week tour to the China mainland with a group of political scientists, Spanish and English were commonly used by many Chinese. Anglos in the Southwest, for the most part, remain monolingual. Historically, they have been surrounded by our culture and language, but to no avail. Even though we live in an area where Spanish has dominated for a long time and where the culture is overcome by the continued presence of people of Mexican origin, many Anglos fail to see the advantages of bilingualism and multiculturalism. Instead, this newer development has become a threat as we can see in our current social environment. Anglos are not the only ones. Many Mexican Americans, particularly the youth, are losing their native language and have become monolingual. It is sad but true.

During my junior year, I was assigned an advisor for the first time in my academic career. I had heard from others about the tirades of Professor Steinbaugh in and out of the classroom. With a low level of confidence, I was not ready to be challenged by him in a classroom setting, but it was my luck to be assigned to him to be my advisor. Dr. Steinbaugh was a great professor with a big heart. He was way ahead of his time in terms of understanding the social inequities and lack of opportunities facing Mexican Americans, particularly Mexican American women. Yet he was boisterous and confrontational. Finally, I met him at his office for advice. He immediately started asking questions.

"What's your name son? Are you from Laredo?" He was not the only one that thought that I was from Laredo. "What is your major, son?"

I proudly told him that it was history.

He said, "I cannot hear you!"

Once again, I replied that my major was history.

Again, he said, "I can't hear you!"

I raised my voice and said, "History!"

"What are you going to do with a major in history?"

My natural response was that I was going to teach.

"Where?" he asked.

The best that I could do was say that I would teach somewhere in South Texas. Once again, he asked me where I would teach, and I said that I did not know specifically. It certainly was not difficult for him to understand that I was clueless in terms of the situation of hiring Latino teachers in Texas and the Southwest.

Then he said, "You don't get it, do you? Do you know that social studies and history are taught by high school coaches?" I said that I did not know. He continued, "It is the god-dammed coaches that teach social studies in the high schools, and they do a lousy job."

I stood there cold! It was clear that I was not truly prepared to make the right decision, nor did I fully understand the realities of racism and the lack of social justice in the school system.

Finally, he said, "Son, just remember that your last name is Villarreal. With this name and coaches teaching history, you will never find a job in this part of the country." He continued to pursue this theme: "Why don't you major in math?"

I replied that I barely passed the required course in algebra.

"What about physics, geometry?" He kept mentioning "hard" sciences until he mentioned biology.

The only thing I could say was that I had good grades in the subject.

"Biology will be your major," he declared. By the way, I had made good grades because of the level of Latin use in biology, and Latin is close to Spanish. I was also able to memorize the intricate parts of plants and the animal kingdom. At that time I did a lot of memory work to buy time, so I could mature and understand the meaning of the work I was doing.

Now I had a double major, and that would require more time. I did not dislike biology, particularly the books and the theoretical side of it. The clinical side of biology was something else. The chemicals in the laboratory, starting with formaldehyde, made me wonder if I could survive and teach in a laboratory. But a job is a job, and I needed one desperately.

In spite of the amount of work that was added, I continued to gain greater confidence in most of the work that I was doing. For example, my ability to be able to relax and appreciate the newer avenues that the university offered inspired in me a better outlook on life and what it can bring. Moreover, greater relaxation greatly contributed to the expansion of my social life, which was also very educational. Going out with friends and acquaintances gave me a greater depth of understanding, not only of the lives of others but also of life in mainstream America. One may think that the political culture of South Texas would be remarkably similar all over South Texas, but it is not. To the contrary, growing up in Laredo is quite different than growing up in Poth, Pawnee, or Hondo. There is a social sophistication among people from Laredo that is never found in people in Poth, Pawnee, or Hondo. As I noted earlier, Mexican Americans from Laredo and other border communities like El Paso suffered far less discrimination than those of us closer to the culture of the Old South and away from Mexico. In Laredo as well as in El Paso, people were far freer than we were on race matters, and having roommates from Laredo gave me some depth of understanding on this social issue.

I am certain that many who were attending university did not change dramatically. To me it was a whole new experience; I was learning new tools, and I was discovering a newer world, which has continued to this day. I believe that these years were the catalyst for an urgency to change, an urgency to learn, and an urgency for new adventures, regardless of age or circumstances. One of my roommates,

Guillermo Rodriguez (Memo), had wide experience in the military. I learned how to cook from him. When he married a beautiful woman from Monclova, Coahuila, he moved out. His replacement was a student in agronomy, a wonderful human being from a small town in South Texas and also a person with military experience. Conrado Vasquez was one of the most dedicated students that I ever met. I studied hard, but not as hard as he did. Like Memo, Conrado also knew about cooking, and it was during these lessons that I began to understand the plight of my mother, my sisters, and women in general. The first time I ate cod fish from a can was with Conrado. What an experience for an inexperienced person!

It was during the last two years of my life at the university that I began to experience an expansion of my social conscience in terms of the many injustices that we impose on each other, particularly the plight of Mexican American women. For minority women who are poor, like my mother, aunts, and sisters, it is far more painful. My gradual and penetrating awareness of this phenomenon started cultivating anger and resentment. This anger and resentment began to turn to a social and political activism that I have maintained throughout my life.

One day as I was driving home from the university for the weekend, I kept thinking about the suffering of poor women who suffer for no reason other than that they are poor and female. I did not have to look far. I had them at home, starting with my mother. Every day they had to endure multiple difficulties and laborious tasks. At the time, two of my sisters were already married with children and out of the house. God knows what they had to go through to survive. But Oralia and Minerva were still at home with Mom and Dad. When I arrived that Friday, I told Mom that I wanted to visit with them since I had something to say. When we got together, I told them point blank that I finally realized their struggles and that from now on I would do everything possible to protect and defend them. I would support their causes regardless of the circumstances. As promised, I have tried throughout my life to defend them in whatever way possible. My two sisters married later in life to two wonderful men, and life was good to them. As I write these notes, I am reminded that only two people are still living from this large family: my sister Oralia, who is living in a nursing home, and me.

The fall semester of 1961 became a critical year in my professional development. Student teaching was the next step to a baccalaureate degree. This involved teaching part-time for a full semester under the supervision of an experienced classroom teacher. My hope was that I would be assigned within the city of Kingsville, since my 1957 Ford Fairlane was in poor shape. When the assignments were made, I was scheduled to be a student teacher in Robstown Junior High. Robstown, which I have known well since my early days when we used to go there to pick onions and cotton, is approximately twenty-five miles away from A&I via Corpus Christi. There were two of us who were assigned to teach at this location, Ignacio (Nacho) Ramos Jr. and me. The distance to drive became less of a problem when I learned who else was going to teach in the same place with me. I was disappointed that Nacho was going to the same place. Rarely do I dislike people, even when some have meant to do wrong, yet I had taken a disliking to Nacho in my few encounters with him. I did not know him well since I never took classes with him (he was a year ahead of me). He came across as arrogant and too full of himself, and on top of that he was *muy agringado* (Anglicized). I remember that on several occasions he would chat with the professors since he knew them well. Nacho was from Kingsville, where his father Ignacio owned a refrigeration store, and many of the professors were his customers. There was a connection that I did not know until later. Anyhow, I thought that it was going to be an unpleasant experience. Nacho was far more affluent than I was. He came from a semi-urban, middle-class family in the city where A&I is located.

It took one single trip to Robstown to change my mind about Nacho. He was and is a super guy with many wonderful qualities, and we have been dear friends for over fifty years. God bless his soul and that of Lydia, his wife!

When I failed my introductory English course, Lydia Hinojosa was in the same class, sitting next to me as I struggled with the course. I sought help from her, but she shied away from me. This and other social circumstances made me suspicious of Lydia, so she was the second person I tried to stay away from since our relations were not good at that moment.

Nacho and Lydia got married a few years later, and I made a special trip to their wedding in December 1964. By then Lydia and Nacho were close friends of mine, and when Norma and I got married six months later in June 1965, they were our *padrinos* (godparents). Since that time Norma and I have had a special relationship with them, a true friendship.

Student teaching at Robstown Junior High was another matter. As much as I like to work with students, I was still very unsure of myself, particularly when I had to speak in a classroom setting. I was fully aware of my accent, and I had to live with it. Nacho seemed to be far better prepared and far more confident. I was assigned to one of the best teachers in the school system, Mrs. Hoover. She had name recognition as a superb and caring teacher; she was amiable, warm but strict, and her students loved her. It was a difficult act to follow. For several weeks I was relegated to a corner, where I made observations. Mrs. Hoover carried her work out with dignity and respect, a classy lady. Yet I think that I exaggerated her talents in my mind since I always felt that other people could do far better than I ever could. The day came when she turned the class over to me, so I could lecture and take care of all matters relating to the classroom. The night before my presentation, I could not sleep since I kept repeating my presentation. The following morning, I arrived somewhat scared but ready to do what I was assigned. I cannot remember what the nature of my presentation was, but I did it three times in a row, since new students would arrive every hour when the bell rang. When I concluded my presentations, I went to see Mrs. Hoover and told her that I thought I had not done a good job. She agreed with me. Mrs. Hoover continued to give me tips and suggestions, and I started to have a better grasp of my assignment. She recommended a passing grade, and by the middle of December, I was finished.

In retrospect, student teaching did me a lot of good. Although I had painful reminders of my past and the problems I had to face to get where I wanted to be, this experience energized me and opened the door to teaching in high school, my long-term goal. What was ahead was subliminal, waiting for something else to happen. I had no idea what. These steps toward maturity and professionalism were coming amid trials and tribulations. I was in the process of turning a corner in my world.

Our old house (located near El Oso Store) where all my siblings were born and raised. Sketch by Carlo Renato Villarreal, 1984.

Sketch of Uncle Gregorio and Aunt Cruz's old house with my double cousins, Ofelia, Gregorio Jr., Chindo, Edelmiro, Alberto, and Gloria, Sketch by Carlo Renato Villarreal, 1980.

My mother (*center*) with some of my siblings at home, circa 1945. *Left to right*: me, my sister Hortencia, my brother Epifanio Jr., and my two sisters Minerva and Oralia.

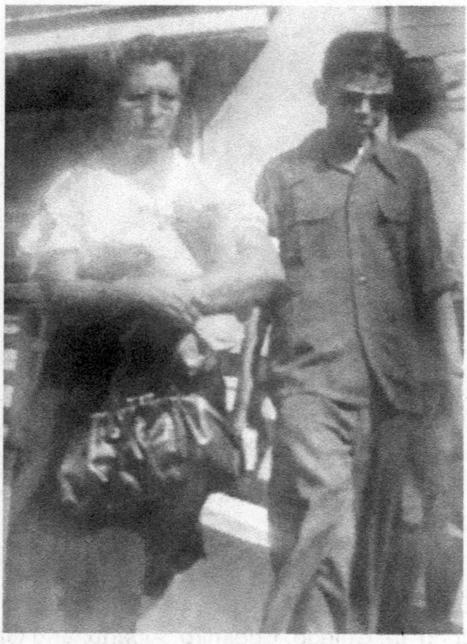

My mother and Epifanio Jr. walking somewhere in West Commerce Street in San Antonio, circa 1948.

Photo of my parents, Maria Antonia and Epifanio Sr., when they were married near El Oso, Texas, 1923.

Virgin de Guadalupe Catholic Church in Pawnee, Texas, where my family attended and attends Sunday services from time to time, 1955.

El Oso baseball team, circa 1947. *Back, left to right*: Tacho, Reynaldo, Jose (umpire), Nino (Tacho's son), and unknown man; *front, left to right*: Genaro (Tacho's son), Carlos, Hilario Jr., unknown man holding unknown child, Remijio, Chema, and unknown man.

El Oso Store, where we purchased most of our groceries, 2024. Near the store was a cotton gin where many community members would bring their wagons with cotton to be ginned.

Hortencia, my sister, and Hilario Jr., her husband, picking cotton at the end of the day in Northwest Texas, 1950.

Three cotton pickers in Northwest Texas, circa 1949. *Left to right*: Carlos (top cotton picker with 1,500 pounds a day), me, and my cousin Remijio, the cotton weigher.

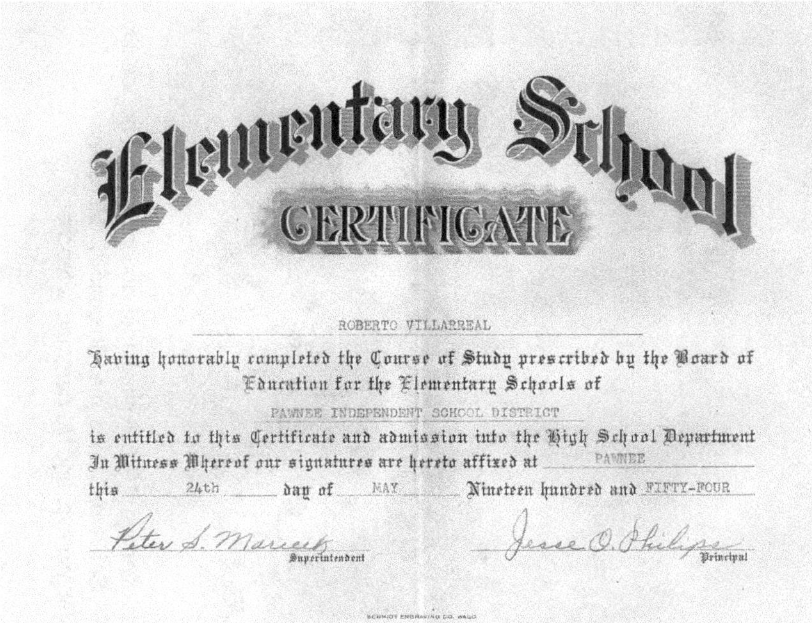

Elementary School
CERTIFICATE

ROBERTO VILLARREAL

Having honorably completed the Course of Study prescribed by the Board of Education for the Elementary Schools of

PAWNEE INDEPENDENT SCHOOL DISTRICT

is entitled to this Certificate and admission into the High School Department

In Witness Whereof our signatures are hereto affixed at PAWNEE

this 24th day of MAY Nineteen hundred and FIFTY-FOUR

Superintendent

Principal

SCHMIDT ENGRAVING CO. WACO

Cadillac Elementary School certificate that I finally earned after twelve years of attending school, 1954.

Cadillac Elementary School, where many of my cousins and friends attended, 1948. A number of students I could not identify. Nevertheless, there are a few I can identify: Issac, David, Seferino, Chindo, me, Gregorio Jr., Mr. Gilley (elementary principal), his daughter Beth, my sister Minerva, and Mr. Bergman, a teacher.

Nell Cemetery, November 2024, where my parents, grandmother, aunts, uncles, cousins, and others are buried. The cemetery is eight miles from where we lived.

My wife Norma, her father Ruperto, and her sister Ethel as new immigrants crossing from Mexico to Eagle Pass, Texas, to live in San Antonio for the first time, 1953.

Our wedding in San Antonio at Santa Cecilia Catholic Church, June 12, 1965. *Left to right*: my sister Minerva, Jose's wife Laurentina, Lydia Ignacio's wife, Amalia, Al's wife, Norma, me, Al, Ignacio, Jose, and Mario.

Left to right: My Uncle Gregorio Sr., my brother Gonzalo, my brother-in-law Hilario Jr., my Uncle Panchito, and my cousin Jesús playing and singing Mexican American ballads near El Oso, Texas, circa 1955.

Old Pawnee High School where I attended the last five years and graduated in 1958. The building is no longer there; it has been replaced by a new middle school.

MRS. THELMA McMUVVEY
First Grade

MRS. ALMA OVERBY
Remedial I

MR. ROGER OVERBY
Jr. High Social Studies, Coach

MR. JESS PHILIPS
Elementary Principal, Sixth Grade
B.S., East Texas State College

MRS. DOROTHY POGUE
Home Economics
B.S., Texas A & I

MR. LACY POGUE
Jr. High English, Algebra
B.S., Texas A & I

MR. ROBERT SHARP
Coach, History
B.S., Howard Payne

MR. L. D. TURNER
Vocational Ag.
B.S., Texas A & I

MR. ROBERT E. VILLARREAL
Remedial II
B.S., Texas A & I

MRS. HOMER WOLFF
Fifth Grade
B.S., U. of Texas

A 1963 photo when I became the first Mexican American to teach migrants in Junior High School in Pawnee. Some members of the faculty were not certified to teach.

Pawnee school reunions were popular as we came together every four years. I had the honor to be the Reminiscent Speaker, the first and last Mexican American. *Left to right*: David Olson, a classmate and high school valedictorian; Joe Cantu, a good friend; and me, 2012.

My father and mother skinning a large pig at home near Pawnee, Texas, 1958. This kind of work was common where nearby groceries stores were not available, and when grocery stores were available, there was no money to purchase the merchandise.

Sociedad Mutualista Benito Juarez in Karnes City, Texas, in the Mexican American barrio, circa 1985. This hall was commonly used for various Mexican celebrations, including 16 de Septiembre, Mexican Independence Day. The hall is still standing but the name has been changed.

Bee County College students preparing a float to represent the College at a parade in downtown Beeville. The float won first place in 1967.

Bee County College student leaders, 1968. *Left to right*: me, Nancy Riggle, Barry Hoff, Lupita Guerrero, and Harry Hingst.

The Poesta Creek Project was an invention of several Bee County College professors and a young Anglo man with the idea to bring the two Beeville communities (Anglos and Mexican Americans) together since the community was divided. Members of both groups were not ready to discuss local issues. The effort died in a matter of months. *Left to right*: an advisor from Trinity University (unknown), Carmen Garza, me, and Ann Green, circa 1973.

Our family in Tuleta, Texas, in 1975. This photo was taken just before we moved to El Paso to join the University of Texas at El Paso. *Back, left to right*: Marco Dante and Carlo Renato; *front, left to right*: my daughter Ethel Minerva, me, and Norma.

A family wedding in Pawnee, Texas, with my brother and sisters and spouses, 1979. *Back, left to right*: Gonzalo, Hilario Jr., Estella, Hortencia, Olga, Adelaido, Leonard, Minerva; *front, left to right*: Lauro and Oralia. Norma and I and Maria and Epifanio Jr. were not able to attend the ceremony.

My family at Cola de Caballo (waterfalls) near Monterrey, Nuevo Leon, circa 1953. *Left to right*: Alicia, Santiago, Mother, Father, me, and Gregorio Jr.

Our children Carlo Renato, Ethel Minerva, her young daughter, and Marco Dante in San Antonio, 1999.

The Monterrey family at a local restaurant in Tomball, Texas, 2015. *Back, left to right*: Carolina Antonia, Sofia Isabel; *front, left to right*: me, Norma, Ethel Minerva, and Valentina Minerva.

President Diana Natalicio commencement introduction with the UTEP administrators, El Paso, Texas, 1994.

Henry Cuellar, the commencement speaker, and UTEP administrators in El Paso, Texas, 1992.

La Fe Clinic located at the center of south El Paso barrio where many poor people obtain medical attention,1986. I can identify a few of its members: Pete Duarte, Alicia Chacon, Enrique Moreno, Hector Holguin, Nicolas Dominguez, and me.

Me at home in our family library near Floresville, Texas, preparing to teach a graduate course to students at the University of Texas–San Antonio, 2015.

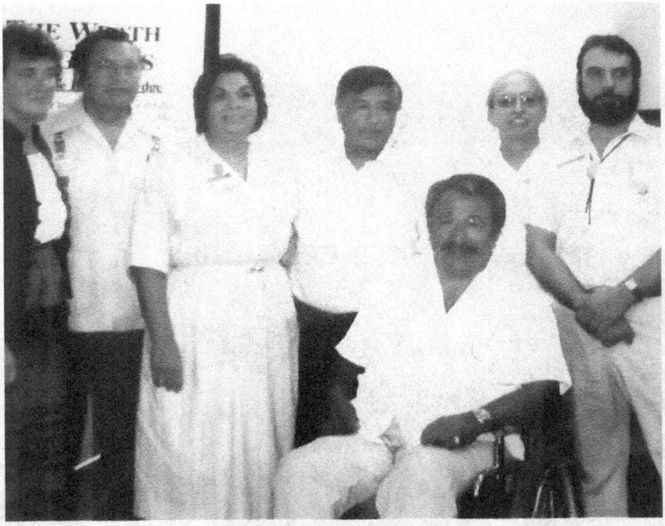

At a workers' union meeting in El Paso, Texas, 1987. *Left to right*: the first and second people are unknown, Alicia, Cesar Chavez, Paul, me, and Victor. Throughout my life I have pursued the interest of the laborer. Although I have spent most of my life in the academic world, my heart remains with the poor workers who earn little but give a lot.

A photo taken after a wedding in San Antonio, circa 1951. The Villarreal and Trevino families of men were celebrating the social event. It is my understanding that their spouses were also celebrating this important event at a different room. I can identify a few members of this party: my father, Epifanio Sr., Francisco, Gonzalo, Adolio, and Alfonso.

At a classroom setting teaching a course in public administration, Theories on Organization and Politics, to the University of Texas–San Antonio graduate students, 2015.

Chapter 6

The Pains of Growing in an Unsettled World

With graduation on the horizon, all the excitement and difficulties of my first degree became something of the past. My plans were to find a job and never bother my parents for money again. I did not, however, have any debts. More importantly, I knew that my time as a full-time student was coming to a screeching halt. I knew that from then on, I was going to have to be a part-time student.

While I was contemplating where to apply, the advice from Professor Steinbaugh kept lingering in my mind regarding securing a teaching job in history in secondary education. Unquestionably, I knew that it was not going to be an easy task to find a job. I spent two weeks trying to write an application letter and researching school directories. There was no doubt that I was a youngster in this business, and I was in for big surprises—surprises that ultimately served me well. I went through countless rejections. One day I had a call from my high school superintendent, Pete Marecek. He told me that there was a position available at the elementary level to teach a group of migrant students ages 6 to 17. The offer was appropriate; after all, I was a graduate from Pawnee, and

I had been a migrant worker for years. I was probably an expert. I was pleased to have a job, and I knew that my mother would be most excited because she wanted to have me, her youngest, at home again.

The summer of 1962 came, and I spent my entire summer working in the fields, waiting for late August to arrive. It was time to go back to the cotton and broomcorn fields to work again, and I did it without a single notion of my new status as a graduate of a university and a junior high teacher. I am certain that I was the only person with a bachelor's degree working in the field in the entire community, including the gringos and everyone else. It was good summer work with a limited social life, as usual, but with great anticipation in terms of my new position in this tiny community. More importantly, however, I was coming home, where I had worked hard with all my anxieties and doubts in terms of having the capacity to do professional work. In the quietest way, I felt triumphant that I had obtained a college degree at a time when some Anglo teachers were teaching without degrees or certificates. It was not the kind of kids I was teaching that bothered me but the social status they had given to the migrant students and me at school. I was given the least esteemed job at the school. Naturally, coming from there, I was sensitive, and I had reasons to be.

Leaving the school where I had always felt inferior four years before, I came to a relationship that had not changed at all. I was put in a lesser position, not because of my qualifications but because of my heritage. I had approximately twenty-three students of different ages. I had to teach them math, history, biology, and everything else. On top of this, I had to teach them in English since Spanish was still not allowed to be spoken at the school, and the students did not know the English language. Undoubtedly, this was the continuation of a formula for failure that had been proven time and again. Under these circumstances, how could a young student manage to overcome these extra barriers and finish school? This was beyond my comprehension. I did it when I was there, but I was defiant and enormously stubborn. I was able to follow my own prescriptions while at least on the surface conforming to the ethos and traditions of the school system. I think that the school policy for migrants was for teachers to do whatever they could and wait for them to drop out. I came to the conclusion that the school policies for migrants were not an option. Instead, I followed the rules as I thought to be practical; after all, I had been a migrant myself.

Lamenting the circumstances and the many reminders of my past, I started working with the students in full dedication. Since no one seemed to care about these students, I did everything I could under the circumstances:

- They were allowed to speak Spanish in class provided the use of Spanish was to communicate while they were making a transition to English.
- They would not follow the old texts given to them since they had limited relevance.
- They would not follow the regular hours scheduled to other students at the school with the hope that they would feel special.
- They would spend more time playing, with the purpose that they would have privileges that other students who were better situated did not have.

I also developed a code of honor in their assignments, complete with new rules and regulations. Fundamentally, the purpose of this endeavor was to begin a process of making these students feel important and that some of the rules of the school would not apply to them. It was fun to work with them, and I certainly became their idol.

I had twenty-three students assigned to me. I knew their parents and families. I certainly hung around with their parents when I was growing up, and there was no social distinction. Many of their parents had gone with us to pick cotton up north; most of them I socialized with, and we participated in the same church and community activities. In other words, their status, their concerns, their environment, and their state of mind was mostly like mine when I was their age. Even though this was years later, not much had changed, as indicative of the serious problems of the education system for the children of migrant workers. No change or any effort to change was the policy of the school system regarding these children. Naturally, the failure rates were extremely high. As far as I know, no student in my class graduated from high school, or even middle school.

Migrants are considered to be in the very outside of the social and educational circle since socially and economically they are at the bottom of the barrel. By the time most students reach school, they know their place in the social system. Few if any would challenge the system to move upward based on this situation. However, I was not looked down on particularly when I was the first Mexican American who taught there. That being said, the surroundings did not help at all. We got the worst room; it was facing the west side where most of the sun hits the large glass windows; the desks were a worn-out compilation of leftovers from other rooms; the room had a closet with an old bookcase with old books totally irrelevant to the students—that was our exclusive library; and the school had left this room without repairs. It was a dump. For migrant students the situation was no different here, at Three Rivers, or at Pharr, Texas. There was a state law that required every student between the ages of 6 and 16 to attend the public school system. So the school responded by providing the least educational and social environment to those who had the most need. The kids were already beaten down, and there was not much to be done other than trying to treat them decently and with respect and trying to find ways to equalize their lives in this hostile environment.

The rural South Texas neighborhood that I was returning to after several years of being away was in some ways not different than the poor neighborhoods in urban areas like San Antonio or Houston at that time. Migrant students had no financial support and no school counseling. Plus, their spoken language and culture were denigrated by a system that associated the Spanish language and the Mexican culture with lesser quality and importance. Historically, the Mexican culture has been viewed as a threat to Anglo Americans, and in some ways this continues. Instead of trying to understand our struggles and strengths, it has been the opposite. For the most part, migrant kids came from decent and organized families; outside the school system, they were not distinguished from the rest of the students or the community. Moreover, most if not all of the students were not on drugs or involved in organized crime like in more urban areas. Most of them had jobs, working in the fields. They were certainly doing well in the community but not in their schools. Urban neighborhoods at that time were home to a variety of problems not found in rural South Texas, such as drugs, organized violence, and lack of work. Yet the rigid social and educational structure and its dated system worked to stigmatize human diversity. There was discrimination, injustice, and an almost total lack of opportunities for students to move up the ladder in the educational world. We would hear expressions by some parents that their kids were not learning or getting anywhere; however, there was no collective way for Mexican Americans to pressure the school system to modify its curriculum and educational culture. Anglo school board members—elected primarily by Anglo voters, school administrators, and schoolteachers—were practically free from any pressure from the Mexican American community. This was true when I attended public schools for sixteen years before I started college. Auspiciously, things have changed over time.

It did not take long for me to make changes in the content of the classroom: I started using the Spanish language since all the students were monolingual, and to avoid punishment, I told them that we would have a nonwritten contract of our internal operations. This was our secretive modus operandi. I completely gave up on the idea of teaching traditionally since the kids would be bored to death. I decided not to abide by the ethos of the school system in and outside of the classroom—in other words, the playground rules. It was common for us to stay on the playground playing baseball while other students and teachers had to go into their classes. The students began to enjoy school, and my relations with them were excellent. The students had never had this experience, and I thought that I had to raise their expectations of themselves if they were ever going to succeed. We thoroughly enjoyed our encounters.

When the spring semester came, I decided to obtain a license to drive an old school bus so I could take them to play softball with others from small rural schools in the area. Among the few schools where we played softball was Coy City. I was their coach, their bus driver, their teacher, and I do not know what else. It was during this time that I met a local teacher who was coaching students at Coy City. Robert H. Thonhoff and I became good friends. As *el otro* (the other) *Roberto*, as he called himself, Thonhoff had extensive knowledge of local history. This was in the spring of 1963, and we have continued to be friends throughout all these years. Years later, when I was a professor in El Paso I had a call from a US ambassador to a tiny country in Africa (a Reagan appointee) asking me if I could come to his home for a gathering on Texas history, focused on the Mexican American War of 1848 in South Texas. He told me that Thonhoff was the speaker for that evening. It was obvious that he knew who I was, and he asked me to be there. I attended the session, and we had a chance to renew our friendship. Moreover, years later, I was reading a Fort Worth newspaper, and I came across a review of one of his books, *The Battle of Medina.* After communicating with the author of the article, I had the opportunity to write an email to Robert (*mi tocayo* or *el otro Roberto*), and he responded quickly. Later, we lived thirty miles away from Karnes City where he lived.

As the fall of 1962 turned into the spring of 1963, several important events had a lasting effect on the rest of my life. It was a memorable year, indeed. Early in the year, John Joshlin, the junior high principal, and I decided to start our master's programs at Texas A&I University. We took turns driving to A&I on Saturdays. We spent the entire spring riding back and forth together, and I accumulated my first six graduate semester hours. The Saturday trips were for more than just advancing my semester hours. John was not from the local area, and that was good news since he did not have the local prejudices or the general suspicion that we faced with local folks. He was a person of considerable experience, and he was struggling with the administration. We had a lot to talk about. I had told him that I wanted to teach either biology or history in high school, and I was looking for an opportunity to do so. I wanted him to keep an eye out for me.

When I was hired at Pawnee, the school had hired a new football and basketball coach. From the very beginning, things did not work for him or the school, and by the end of the fall semester, he was fired. The coach, as Steinbaugh had predicted, was teaching social sciences. Joshlin told me that it was a perfect move for me, so I proceeded to apply in February 1963. My eternal optimism told me that I had a chance. Nothing was said about my application throughout the spring semester. Meanwhile, I was asked to replace him as the coach of the basketball team. I did a lousy job, and we finished early since we lost practically every game. In the spring of 1963, I had two coaching jobs, basketball for the school and softball for the migrant students.

I never heard from anyone about my application for this new position, and suddenly May arrived and school was almost over. I ask John to inquire about the status of my application. After some investigation he came back and told me that the job had already been given to someone else. There was no courtesy call, nor a letter of thanks for applying. Nada! Frankly, it was common practice in those days that if a Mexican American applied for a position, there was simply no courtesy to reply. These issues were handled in a very unprofessional way. I decided that it was time to visit with Pete Marecek, the superintendent. He apologized for what had been done, and he constructed his side of the conversation to make it appear as if he was on my side. The school board, he said, was not ready for me. He was frank and open. He said, "Robert, the board is not ready to hire a Mexican American to teach in high school; I am sorry." He told me that it would take another ten or twenty years for that to happen. Once again, he apologized. I looked at him straight in his eyes and told him that I was resigning from my position. He asked me if I had another position and I told him that I did not. He said that he felt sorry, but the decision stood.

As I drove home, I kept thinking about my parents, particularly my mother. How was I going to tell her the bad news? I got home and told my mother that I was resigning from my job. My poor mother stood speechless. After she paused, she told me to do whatever was good for me, but she warned me that the military was still after me. It was a sad day for my mother, father, and sisters since they knew that I was now leaving and probably for good. This was the end of the line. It was a sad occasion for me, too, since I cared a lot for them, and this was my second and final departure as far as living at home. Even after many years, I still feel bad for them. *Pero asi es la vida!* (That is the way life was meant to be!)

Early spring of 1963 was a busy time for me. I had my first experience of taking graduate courses at Texas A&I University. For the first time in the history of our family, the middle school principal came to see my family (while I was in bed with the mumps). And I heard Mama telling us some folks were coming from San Antonio to visit us. Let me expand this long story. Alfonso Treviño, my brother Gonzalo's brother-in-law and his wife, Amanda, were bringing the Pedrazas home. When Sunday came, Alfonso and Amanda arrived with the new visitors. By the time they arrived, Mama had prepared lunch, so we were waiting for them. We met Ruperto and Manuelita Pedraza at our home. Who were they? There is a long and beautiful story behind all of this. When my mother and her four brothers were living in Nuevo Laredo, Mexico, they knew Ruperto. Although he was far younger than my mother, he thought highly of her, thinking that she was the most beautiful person he had ever met. At this point we learned that my mother's brother, Santiago had married Ruperto's only sister, Bernarda. I did not know all of this. I knew Tia Bernarda because she would come with Tio Santiago to visit us, or we would go to Monterrey to visit with them, but nothing beyond that. Before the Pedrazas left, they told us that they had two daughters, Norma and Ethel. The visit was pleasant and eventful. A few weeks later I was told that Peto (Ruperto) and Manuelita were coming back to see us. Well, in the next trip I was surprised that Norma and Ethel came with them. I was told later that they did not want to come, but their father put his foot down. We had a formal and wonderful time since the Pedrazas' mannerisms were elaborate and proper as compared with our rural lifestyle. Fundamentally, the Pedrazas and we belonged to a different class structure. Ceremony and parsimony were some of the Pedrazas' strengths. During this visit I took some time to visit with Norma as we took a stroll down to the corrals where the pigs and sheep were kept. I took a liking to her, and I asked myself how I was going to approach this girl. They left, and I could tell that my parents were most satisfied with the visit. For days I kept thinking about Norma, so I decided to write her a thank-you note for the visit, and she responded with a similar message. We continued to communicate until gradually I worked up the courage to ask her for a date, and she agreed. It never occurred to me at this point that she would ultimately be my future wife and that Ruperto and Manuelita would be my *suegros* (parents-in-law). I was truly fortunate!

I continued my graduate classes during the summer while I continued looking around for a new position. Finally, in the last few days of summer, I found a position teaching biology at Pharr–San Juan–Alamo High School in the Lower Rio Grande Valley. From then on I would come home once a month. On one of those trips, I told my mother that I was planning a trip to San Antonio to visit with Norma, and I also told my mother of my intentions. Mother was pleased but concerned that this new relationship could potentially ruin the relationship they had established with the Pedrazas. She asked me to behave well and act like a gentleman. I promised that I would and told her not to worry about it.

The monthly weekend trips from the Valley were made directly to my house on Friday evening and then on to San Antonio on Saturday afternoon. I would stay overnight in a cheap three-dollar motel down on South Presa Street, then I would have lunch with Norma. Soon I would be driving to Pawnee to prepare for the trip back to the Rio Grande Valley. My first visitation with the Pedraza family was most formal; I was on my best behavior, as I wanted this relationship to be lasting. In many ways my future wife and I are very different socially since we grew up in very different social environments. Culturally, however, our backgrounds are similar. During my overnight stays in

San Antonio, for example, I would get up early on Sunday, get ready, and go out to have breakfast by myself at Capt. Jim's. Norma would sleep late. Then after breakfast, I had to wait a long while before I arrived at her house close to eleven in the morning, so she was awake. I did not mind this, but I found it hard to believe since at home everybody would get up early regardless of what day of the week it was. Anyway, the first day, I arrived at the Pedrazas' house, and her dad asked me to come in and visit with him in the living room. I was impressed with their house and the way they maintained it. After a short while, Norma showed up. We visited for a while, and I noticed that Señora Pedraza was not around. I inquired and was told that she was sick that day and was in bed. I asked Norma if I could visit her since I thought that it was prudent to do that. She showed me the way to her room, and I visited with her for a moment before leaving for a memorable first date. I learned later why my future mother-in-law was "sick": because Norma was going out with me. She did not like the idea at all. Soon life got better and she became a wonderful mother-in-law.

During the summer of 1963, before I got the job in Pharr–San Juan–Alamo school, I had a call from Cristina Treviño. I did not know Cristina well beyond the fact that she had married a distant member of the family. She had learned about my situation, and she came to my assistance. She told me to come to San Antonio and she would personally take me to various locations to apply. Cristina and I spent two solid days together, going from place to place, applying for teaching positions. Once again, the well was dry, the month of August was upon us, and the Army was waiting for me. This bothered me, not because I was trying to avoid the military, but because of my mother's resistance to seeing another son go to war. Just before summer school ended, there was an opening in the Pharr–San Juan–Alamo school district, and I sent in an application. I solicited the help of one of my professors, and two weeks later I was invited for an interview for a position at the high school. They desperately needed biology teachers. I went for the interview just four days before school was to start. In the interview the superintendent was not conclusive since he felt that my "Mexican" accent was unacceptable. I welcomed the culture of the Rio Grande Valley, but the level of racism was pronounced.

Going to teach in a large high school in the heart of the Rio Grande Valley was a new experience. I was excited since at this juncture of my career, teaching social sciences in high school was my goal and dream. To become a high school teacher in a sizeable high school was something very special. I would never have imagined being able to do this, particularly when I was attending Pawnee High School. My relations with the faculty at Pharr–San Juan–Alamo were smooth and comfortable. We supported each other without any trouble. Yet there was an ethnic division that consistently separated us. The best approach was for me to act like everything was fine, and there was no discussion of our ethnic and cultural differences. My relations with the students were good. Yet quietly, and not so quietly, some of the Anglo students, particularly the more affluent ones, were somewhat perturbed by the authority of a teacher of Mexican origin. They were not used to having Latino teachers telling them what to do. There was a certain level of silence and understanding, and life went on like nothing was happening.

Coming to the Valley gave me the opportunity to become more socially active, and I began to make this experience more compatible with the professional tasks before me. I took full advantage of this adventure. By the time I moved to the Valley, I was already dating Norma, but I was also active in Valley activities. The social experience was fantastic. I learned to appreciate better what I had, I acquired social maturity, and I learned to better integrate with a remarkably diverse group of people. These skills were learned in the name of fun and entertainment.

When I came to the Valley, I felt very much at home. Socially speaking, the place was warm, fluid, and more culturally to my liking. Yet it seemed that the class structure was more rigid and vertical, but at least there were some elements of middle-class life among the Mexican Americans. My cultural background paralleled this cultural environment. At the other end of the spectrum, I was part of the school system, and it was rare for Mexican Americans to be teachers. That was my initial break. The institutions and processes were all Anglo, and they had a firm grip on all aspects of social, political, and educational life in these institutions.

The faculty at Pharr–San Juan–Alamo was a mixture of old-timers, local teachers, and a few sprinkles of new faculty from outside the area. This distinction is important because there were considerable differences in social attitudes between local folks and recent newcomers. The Rio Grande Valley high school reflected the established social conditions of "them" and "us." There was a social and ethnic line that kept us apart. It has always been my job to try to break barriers that are motivated by prejudice. We owe this to those who are coming behind us, regardless of their background and social status in life. To test the waters after a month of being part of the school system, I asked Ann, an Anglo woman from East Texas, if we could go out and have dinner together. Without hesitation she accepted the invitation. The day that we were to visit, she gave me a call and told me that she had to cancel and gave me an excuse. Knowing the contemporary social conditions, I knew the social problem. She soon called and told me that her landlord advised her not to do it since it would hurt her reputation. Ann got scared and backed out. Crossing the ethnic line was still very questionable. A time will come when this barrier will be put behind us, and it already has to a certain extent.

In June 1965 I married Norma Pedraza Aguirre. My life changed, especially when we had our first child, Marco Dante, who was born in the Rio Grande Valley. When I met Norma, she was full of life and working full-time as a manager of a women's clothing store in downtown San Antonio. She had arrived here from Saltillo with her parents and sister, stopping first in Ozona, Texas, then moving later to San Antonio in 1953. I was fortunate to marry a person of many great qualities, including decency, loyalty, and dedication to our kids, our families, and me. She has dedicated her life to the many endeavors that the family and I have been involved in for the benefit of all of us.

In the spring of 1966, I started preparing to finish my master's degree. At that moment in time, like before, I was thinking about my next step. A doctoral degree sounded good, so I started applying to graduate programs in different places across the nation, including one Ivy League university. Soon after our first child was born, I resigned from my teaching position and launched myself into pursuit of a doctoral degree. In a matter of four years, I had resigned from my second professional position, and I no longer had a job. The purpose behind acquiring a doctoral degree was not necessarily to get a job or to have a higher position or prestige. My sentiment and obligation were to break the barriers set by others who found it advantageous to keep us in "our place." Based on this situation, I had my parents in mind. Whatever I could do to make a difference, I was most willing to do it. What better way than by getting the ultimate degree that a university has to offer? Since early childhood, I have had an obsession with changing existing conditions, conditions that have suffocated minority groups, including women. Throughout my life, I have always had a burning desire to try to diminish the barriers that have prevented me from reaching my goals. This mental struggle was so profound that I gradually fell into a depression. It was a painful process. Fear of the unknown overpowered me. I enjoyed talking to crowds, but unknown fears made my life miserable. My inability to handle these struggles took me on a spin, and it lasted for years.

By the early 1960s, political activism began to give me a new and enduring perspective. By this time in my life, ethnic and racial challenges had truly taken hold of me. I could not let them go. I felt that education and political activism were the way to fight the high level of discrimination that existed against minorities, particularly for people of Mexican origin. Despite my full commitment to bringing about change, I felt unprepared since I was coming from a nonpolitical environment that supported the status quo. That would change.

I thought the best tool to acquire was formal education, and I chose political science as a profession, not knowing the difference between practical and theoretical politics. I would need to excel, and education was the way to do it. Other people with a better grasp of the world of politics would probably have taken a different road. Under the circumstances, I could not see any other avenues. I rushed into a world that I had little understanding of, but I was willing to pay whatever price was necessary to obtain what I wanted. A doctoral degree in political science from an American university was my goal. It was not until much later that a colleague and friend of mine, Dr. Melvin P. Straus, told me in conversation that I was a "man of destiny who never shies away from seeking and protecting a newer world." Learning and practicing politics were the tools to get there. I promised myself that I would take every step necessary to provide a more dignified experience for Mexican Americans who had to suffer the consequences of a society in which people of color were not welcomed.

Chapter 7

The Trials and Tribulations of Transitions

Like many of my compatriots, central to my goals was to challenge the socioeconomic and political divide by pursuing higher education. To pursue this goal, I resigned two teaching positions without having another job, without having any major material resources, and with an additional member in our family to support. My enthusiasm for pursuing new adventures was so overwhelming that not having a job seemed not to be of great concern. I knew I could survive if I had an understanding with my wife and family. As always, my wife and family were persistently supportive, and that made a huge difference. Meanwhile, I kept preparing myself with hope that I would find a good school not too far away.

Unlike when I applied for a teaching position for the first time, where school administrators did not have the courtesy to formally respond, this time I had responses from a variety of universities, including Princeton. Going to Princeton was not within my budget, nor did I want to go that far away from my family. It would have been a great sacrifice for my wife, son, and immediate family. Nevertheless, it was a boost for my ego, and I needed it. More importantly, I wanted to prove to myself and to others that I was just as good as anyone and that I was just as qualified to enter several universities, *chingonas* (big), as my cousin Remijio used to say. I chose the University of Oklahoma, and to this day I am grateful to the faculty who taught me there and to the university itself. It was an experience that had long-lasting effects.

With the assistance of my two brothers, after three years living in the Rio Grande Valley, we were packing up all of our belongings in an old truck. The time had come to leave the Valley behind and start a new adventure. This trip, more than before, was truly adventurous. Our first child had just been born, we had no saving to support ourselves, I was borrowing money to attend the university, and Norma was staying with her folks in San Antonio. But our spirits were high, and we were optimistic that, in the long run, we would be doing very well. Obviously, there were many questions that needed to be answered. But these questions were put to the side without many worries.

Naturally, I turned to my family. For example, while Norma was resting at a hospital after the birth of our first child, my mother-in-law and I went to a clothing store in McAllen to look for an overcoat in preparation for the trip to Norman, Oklahoma. What's more, Manuelita was going to take care of our young child while my wife went to work in San Antonio. The company gave Norma back the job that she had left a year earlier when we married. These changes allowed me to attend the university.

My wife and I enjoyed the company and help from my brothers. In our short stay with my parents, I noticed that my mother appeared not to be in the best of health. She looked tired and exhausted. My sister Olga was generous to let us use one of her small houses so we could store our belongings. Once we unloaded our belongings, we moved north. Gonzalo treated us to barbecue in Karnes City. Another big assistance came from our *padrinos* (by marriage), Al and Amalia Marsh, who were generous to cosign a loan for me. The loan and a small scholarship from the university gave me the opportunity to attend the first year.

Resigning from reliable jobs, the birth of our first child, and leaving my wife and child behind with limited resources put extensive pressure on our families. To their credit, no one ever made any comments to us. Moreover, for generations our family had lived very close together, within a mile or two from each other. To my parents, having their children living nearby was critical since they were ready to help them. We would help them, too. We had a long tradition of helping each other in all matters.

I unwillingly broke all the rules in search of a dream that was hard to explain since obtaining a PhD in political science must have seemed insignificant to my entire family. Paradoxically, and ultimately, my intentions in seeking a doctorate were to honor my parents for all their struggles. I wanted the family to make a difficult transition from the lower to the middle-class, to prove to the community of Anglos that we could reach these new heights, and to show that discrimination and lack of access to resources and opportunities were gradually becoming a thing of the past. Although this transformation took a toll on all of us, I like to believe that I was part of a group spearheading this long-range drive.

I have been misunderstood in terms of who I am and what I have become. I believe that I display an image to my family and community that is unrealistic. In my early school years, I lived in two distinct worlds—home and school—for a long time. In the process I became a master of not disturbing either world. At school I was shy, quiet, and subordinate. At home I was myself just as much as my siblings. As time went on, the gap between my family and me widened. Still, I was able to bridge the gap and continue to be the same person that I was when I grew up with my brothers and sisters. My professional growth was not part of the family and community. The purpose of this effort was not to alienate either my family or the community. Instead, I wanted to be part of them, and I thought that the path I had chosen was the way to accomplish this mission. Norma to this day claims that neither side of the family really knows me.

Dealing with a multitude of change put me on the road for a mental depression that lasted for years. Gradually, I withdrew from people, and fear took control of me. I started having trouble eating (swallowing), and I was terrified of the students in my classroom. I did not know why, nor I could identify solutions. This was a real paradox since I love people. I love my students, and I enjoy the limelight. As the depression worsened, I did two things: I learned how to deal with it since I appeared relaxed and as though I was enjoying my work. Inside, it was another story, a story of horrible inner conflicts capped with phobias. The second effort on my part was not to seek drugs to cure the pain. I learned to stay cool and provide a warm smile. This became my trademark. I think that people wondered how I could deal with a difficult and complicated world when I gave the appearance of being soft and not strong enough to deal with hard issues. Norma knew better since she always claims that my appearance and demeanor are quite different than my actions and determination.

On the surface life went smoothly as I handled my many new tasks with confidence and determination. Although I was afraid of my immediate surroundings without knowing why, somehow, I had the determination to do whatever it would take to complete my tasks despite a mental illness that never ceased to exist. For example, when I had to orally participate in a classroom or talk to a group of people, I was thrilled to do it, but from the moment that I learned that I had to make such presentation, I was in the state of fear. It was a serious contradiction that lasted for approximately twenty years of my professional life. What a nightmare! The good side of this is that it taught me, like my childhood struggles, a lot about life and the pains and difficulties that people have to go through. I now live without those fears and anxieties, and life has become most enjoyable and complete.

I arrived at the University of Oklahoma in early September 1966 with high expectations. Finally, I was a doctoral student. I stayed in university housing for one semester, but it was too expensive. I moved to less expensive housing that was closer to the university. During the semester Norma and my son came to visit me. It was a joy to have them there.

I had my hands full with twelve semester hours of graduate courses. Just as I had experienced the difference between high school and university, I had a similar experience when I entered University of Oklahoma. The Department of Political Science was well established with professors at the top of their field. It was a tough but beautiful experience to be working on a doctoral degree with a group of talented professors and students. I truly dedicated my whole life to studying and learning the culture of the university. The expectations for students were high, and I tried to perform well. At the end of the semester, I managed to pass with good grades. At that time the fall semester ended in mid-January instead of early December. I spent most of the holidays catching up and finishing research assignments. In one of the courses, I had to type over one hundred pages. Thanks to my niece, Maria Elena Chapa, who helped enormously by typing a lengthy paper before the deadline. Rest in peace, dear Maria Elena.

When I moved to a new apartment, I was joined by a new roommate. Christus had come from Greece in hopes of earning a bachelor's degree. A highly spirited and friendly guy, he was carefree and careless with a touch of fatalism. I was introduced to Greek wine and olive oil, among other experiences. For the spring I had a demanding curriculum, but I had a good handle on it. Although spring started well, soon it became clear to me that living apart from my wife and child was difficult for her and for me, and in the long run, it would be counterproductive. I started running out of money, and the prospects of getting a job at the university were nonexistent. Still, having a feeling of being lesser than others, I kept a distance from the faculty and graduate students. This was a mistake. I learned a hard lesson that I corrected when my family and I returned to the University of Oklahoma three years later.

As I said earlier, when I left to go to the university, my mother was not looking well. As time went on, her health continued to deteriorate.

This was a serious concern for the entire family since Mama was everything to us. That was one of the hardest experiences of my life. In April my sister Lala called and told me that Mama was gravely ill. I immediately prepared to come home. For the first time in my life, I flew on an airplane. By the time I arrived at the hospital, Mama was in a coma, and she died soon after. Mama played a central role in our family, and the depth of her absence was far greater than we had ever anticipated. My father was lost without her, the spirit of the family was partially gone, and the relations of the family changed forever. I was devastated. I continue to miss her daily, though she died more than sixty years ago, on April 20, 1967. Soon after the funeral, I flew back to Oklahoma City to continue my studies.

Upon returning to the University of Oklahoma, I had one month to wrap up the semester. I managed my classes well, and I kept earning good grades. I knew that I could not stay any longer; I needed to find a job. One evening I got a telephone call from Peter Marecek, the superintendent of the Pawnee schools. The last time I had talked to Pete was when I resigned my position after being told that I was not qualified to teach high school because of my ethnic background. He told me that there was a new college in Beeville that was planning to open its doors for the fall semester of 1967. He asked if I would consider becoming a faculty member, telling me I would be a great asset to this new college. He had been elected as a board member, and he said he would be glad to talk to the president of the college about a position for me. I let him know that I was interested and that I would visit the president and the dean of the college as soon as I could. When the spring semester was over, I drove to Beeville for an interview. The interview was pro forma. I was given a tour of the college by the newly hired dean. We went back to the office, and they had a contract ready for me to sign. This was the beginning of a new era in my adventure to reach the top. I immediately called Norma and told her the good news, and it became clear that our second son, Carlo Renato, was going to be born in Beeville, Texas. I was starting the second year of my doctoral program, but it had to wait.

As an introduction to becoming a new college faculty member, I was selected for a summer program at the University of Texas at Austin. It was a delightful opportunity to meet others who were also becoming involved in higher education. Besides this assignment, I took two graduate courses in government with the understanding that I could transfer them to University of Oklahoma. We stayed at a girls' dorm near the university, and the stipend covered room, board, and travel. It was easy to travel on weekends from Austin to San Antonio. Yet the premature death of my mother created an unsettling vacuum. At the University of Texas, I met Gus Dunn, who was going to be the chair of the Social Studies Department. Gus was an experienced, older, and wealthy man whose father was once president of Clark University when the internationally famous psychologist Sigmund Freud came to speak on his theories on psychoanalysis. Gus was everything: He was a faculty member, he preached on Sundays in his hometown (over three hundred miles away from the college), he was a farmer with a lot of land, he was an owner of a Massey-Ferguson tractor dealership, and he was a world traveler. Gus was a person with an enormous amount of energy and a desire to work. He was flamboyant, always wearing a tuxedo and a black bowler hat and carrying an excessive amount of money in his pocket. His wife Gretchen was far younger than he, and he always introduced her as his "Secretary of War and Treasure." He once had supported Grady Hogue, the new president at the college, for a state senate race. With all these assets, however, he was just a small-town operator and politician, and a somewhat narrow-minded human being. He took a liking to me, and we spent a lot of time together traveling, eating, and visiting. Sometimes he was fun to be around, and sometimes he could be an embarrassment.

I completed the courses at the University of Texas, and I was ready to move my family to Beeville. Unfortunately, the housing situation was very tight. After two days of hunting in this small town, I found a house out in the country about eight miles from the city. I called Norma and gave her news about the housing situation. Norma balked at the idea of living outside the city limits. To her the city was small by itself, and now we had to go to a farm. I could not convince her since her fears took precedent. The only solution I could find was to buy a new house, and we did. I was against the idea because I was planning to return to the University of Oklahoma, and buying a house made it more complicated. Like it or not, I became the proud owner (with all its debts) of a new home on the east side of Beeville, near where the president of the college lived.

Norma resigned her job and started her life as the wife of a professor. The school opened in early September, and by midweek Hurricane Beulah hit this small community. We made a quick transition to San Antonio. When we came back after the storm, the house was still intact after more than thirty inches of rain. The storm did a lot of damage to the community.

With the intensification of moving to this community, I could not prevent myself from becoming part of the political community. I wished that I had more experience, but it was never too late to learn—and learn I did. As the Civil Rights Movement intensified, I decided to concentrate on writing my dissertation. As a practical matter, the community of Bee County became the topic and focus of my dissertation. During the next three years of political and social turmoil, I wrote the dissertation. The study analyzes the social and political strife between Anglos and Mexican Americans as the minority group struggles for justice and equality. The changes of this movement were minor in substance. The impact never fully matured. This created a lot of frustration and discontent within the Latino community. Being second-class citizens was deeply ingrained in our consciousness, and challenging the Anglos, for the most part, was a foreign concept. Unsurprisingly, the Mexican American community was divided on the issue of political mobilization. To older people who had suffered the consequences of discrimination and the few middle-class Hispanics, political change meant a whole lot of trouble. As much as they wanted to gain power, the risks were too high, and while there was a spark of fire among the younger crowd, the risks to their status were too great to challenge the political culture of the community at that time.

Very few Mexican Americans were willing to risk their economic and political lives to bring about change. Notwithstanding all the failures, this social and political upheaval had future consequences. The power of Latinos felt short, and the process of moving up was slow at best. However, for all practical purposes, a group not in power was challenging the establishment. This became enormously alarming when, in a local election, Beeville Chicanos won all the city council positions. It served as a major threat to Anglos since the potential for a political explosion was not beyond possibility. The president of the college, a politician, became worried, and he would call me and ask questions. I could tell that like other Anglos, he was fearful. When I went back to Oklahoma, I put this turmoil behind me and focused on finishing my degree.

Because of my unique status in the community, I was invited just about everywhere, even to lunches at the country club. I was the guest speaker and keynote speaker at several events, some of them at the local naval base. The subjects chosen for these events were touchy and controversial, such as bilingual education, ethnic and racial minorities, and the La Raza Unida movement. I was familiar with these topics, but the audiences had no appreciation for them. Instead, their hope was to stop or eradicate any momentum for change. At one of these events, the president of the college called and asked me if I could speak to the Rotarians at the local country club. The speaking engagement was on bilingual education in Texas. In my presentation I took a broad view of some of the advantages of bilingualism and why we should take a hard look at and debate the issues. The question-and-answer session focused on how to do away with programs focused on bilingualism. From the Rotarians' perspective, bilingual education would keep Mexican Americans from entering the educational mainstream, slow down their learning of the English language, and retard their overall progress. In José Limon's study of *Americo Paredes*, there are discussions on the infringement of Anglos to keep Chicanos from growing to full potential.

As I elaborated on this subject, it became increasingly clear to me that I would pay for the honor of these frequent speaking engagements. Frankly, at the early stage of this saga, I had no idea what I was getting into—neither in the community nor at the college. I would learn better as time went on. In many ways I was enjoying it, but I was unprepared for this honor. I became both the pride and threat of higher education in this small community. I had a lot of support, but it came from the students and the Mexican American community, not from the conservative elite that started with the president of the college. Yet as much as the president of the college was threatened by the coming of bilingual education, when money became available, he acquired a grant and hired Anglo teachers to teach Spanish.

One of the great experiences in starting a new college is that new traditions can be set. One of the most rewarding extracurricular activities to me was serving as an advisor to the new Student Government Association. There were two things especially important in this new venture: great students and the opportunity to learn and work with the students as they worked to establish new traditions that are still in existence. The student leadership promoted several ideas that were part of the bylaws of student governance, but we went beyond that. Out of the blue came the idea to invite speakers to come to campus. As a new college, we were incredibly attractive to speakers, who would come at a low cost. One of the speakers, for example, came with his wife and spent the night with us to avoid hotel expenses. We brought in several outstanding speakers, including Congressman Henry B. Gonzalez. My relations with the student leaders (particularly the Anglos) were superb. We trusted each other, and the ethnic and racial barriers practically disappeared. This was, however, not true of the faculty.

This was an enjoyable and gratifying venture until I ran into trouble with the president of the college. As I became a popular figure on campus, glorified by some of the student leaders, the president became concerned. I was becoming a threat. Under the political environment that we were in at the time, it did not take much to threaten the president. As a political figure, the president was suspicious of anyone who gained attention and popularity. This popularity peaked when we invited Congressman Henry B. Gonzalez to speak. He arrived late to a full crowd in the college auditorium. Although he was almost two hours late, the people never left. His presentation was specific on certain aspects of our economy. We had dinner at eleven that night, and his assistant drove him back to San Antonio. The next morning I had a call from the president of the college. I thought that he was going to congratulate me on our success. Well, this was just naivety on my part. He said that he was worried about the speakership series because we could bring "unacceptable" and "radical" people to campus. Therefore, from now on, he would have to approve each speaker. I told him that the series of speakers that we had chosen were not of that ideology, that the students and community were very receptive, and that I had considerable trust in the judgment of our students. Besides, I was doing this on a voluntary basis for the betterment of the college. Without further say, I resigned as student advisor.

In the operational process, it became clear to me that my desire to acquire freedom and responsibility was colliding with the local authorities, who had a long tradition of authoritarianism. The concerns about my campus activities were not limited to our president. There were elements of the faculty that were distrustful and fearful of my activities, and they were looking for ways to contain me. I think their fear was that politically, I was using the students. This was an excuse. The real reason they showed skepticism and distrust was that I represented a group in the community (or at least the leadership, thank goodness!) that was beginning to raise their voices to seek representation and justice. Representation and justice are very scary to some folks.

One day I was busy in my office preparing for a lecture when one of my colleagues, a biology professor, came to visit me. At that time Henry was the president of the Texas Association of Community Colleges. I learned later that he was brought in by the president of the college as a star professor. Henry had the appearance of being shy and rather quiet. As soon as he got there, he started to make accusations. For a moment I thought that he was joking since the comments were completely off the wall. He told me that I did not belong in the college; I was a lowly cotton picker that belonged out in the fields of South Texas; and he claimed that I was not a good Christian, and he felt sorry for my wife and kids for having me as a husband and father. Before he started conversing, I asked Henry if he would sit down, but he refused, standing in the doorway while he made all these comments. Some of my colleagues came to my rescue soon after Henry left. One of my colleagues said, "I cannot believe that Henry would say that!" I explained my views to my colleagues that I was used to this kind of treatment since in my early years I had received a lot of insults. They asked me if I was planning to do something, and I said no. I would just let it go.

Later that day I received a call from the president of the college. He wanted to visit with me. I went to his office with the understanding that he probably had heard about Henry's conversation, and I was right. Grady Hogue asked me if Henry and I had had an encounter that morning. I responded affirmatively. He said, "Henry is a good man, he is the current president of the Texas Association of Community Colleges, and I am sure that he means nothing negative about you." I was now being insulted again, so I immediately countered his allegations by saying that he brought me to his office to insult me again. I said that it was obvious that he had his preferences, and I was not the guy he preferred. So I said, "I don't want any more of this." At that point I started walking out of his office, and that was the end of the conversation.

Years later I was hired by the University of Texas at El Paso as a university professor. While I was clearing out the office that I had occupied for years as director of the Federal Programs, Henry appeared at the door. We said hello to each other, and I asked him if I could be of assistance. He said, "No, I just want to wish you well in your new adventure. You're a better man than I am." He turned around and left the office. I never saw Henry again until many years later, when the president of the college, John Brockman, invited us for dinner one evening.

Sometimes, without intent, I would gravitate to the turbulent waters that often brought change. Naively, my goal when I chose higher education was to free myself of the many prejudices I encountered in the community. At Bee County College, I sought space so I could participate, but that was not possible. For example, the faculty could not meet unless the president was present. I asked around, and I was told that this was the way business was conducted. I could not believe it. I was coming to an institution of higher learning to get away from the eternal control of the administration on faculty that is so present in public schools. So a group of faculty members met to discuss the feasibility of finding an answer to this most undemocratic practice in academia. Out of these meetings came the idea of organizing a faculty senate to discuss issues pertaining to the faculty. We decided to inquire at more mature colleges and universities to formulate something useful at our college. When it came down to signing the letter, however, every member of the group decided not to sign the letter. We were heading for trouble. I was the only faculty member that signed the letters to approximately ten different colleges and universities across the state. As we began to receive information, I got a call from the president. I knew that I was in hot water since every time he called me it was to reprimand me for my activities.

In my visit to the president, he had a letter that I had mailed. "Robert, I got a letter from an old friend from Temple Community College, and it has your signature. Did you write this letter?" My response was affirmative. Grady pursued the matter further: "Robert you are a good man, and I cannot believe that you did this since this is destructive to our good institution." I told him why I was doing it. Faculty and administration have different issues and problems. Faculty needs the freedom to advise the administration. He received this message like a ton of bricks had fallen on him. He continued: "Who is behind this idea? It certainly was not you." I told him that I had done it. Grady knew better. He told me that he was going to talk to other suspects and get to the bottom of this volatile and controversial issue. After several months of investigation, one of my colleagues from the English Department was fired. I continued to think that he would not fire me. There was a problem in firing the only Hispanic faculty member at the College. We were in the midst of a political war between the Anglo and Mexican American communities, and to fire the only Mexican American faculty was counterproductive. It would add fuel to the fire, and Anglos were working on the pacification of the community. Not only that, but I had not done anything but to up the status of the college.

The president would never take big risks. He was not an educator, nor was he hired to be an educator. He was a small-town politician at a community college that was well connected with some legislators around the state. His job was to bring money to the school. There was no question that by the standards of the community, he was a powerful figure. He knew some of his limitations, and firing the only Latino faculty member in the college was not part of the act. As a person, I had no trouble with him, nor did I plan to attack him in any way. What I was trying to do was to change matters that were detrimental to the faculty.

I came to Bee County College unprepared to deal with the politics of the college and community. I had no experience or training. My focus was to teach for the first time in higher education. My intent did not last long. Upon arrival I became a celebrity to the Mexican American leadership and Anglos for different reasons. For the leaders of the Mexican Americans, I knew how desperate they were. They were reaching out to anyone who could give them a helping hand. Suddenly, I found myself in a new role that I had never dreamed of. It became a sizeable dilemma. We were new in the community, and my wife was expecting our second child. The rigors of starting to teach in higher education were particularly hard. As the only minority person in the faculty, I had to do twice as much as others to sustain my role and be acceptable and functional in a new situation.

Members of the new college remained silent regarding the struggles between Latinos and Anglos in the community. Nevertheless, a few faculty in the social sciences were willing to commit themselves in some way to become involved in the community. Our involvement was going to be nonpolitical. The Poesta Creek, located where the two communities were divided, became the place to bring Anglos and Mexican Americans together. A history professor represented the college, and a young Anglo man represented the Anglo community. A professor from Trinity University in San Antonio was invited to be the moderator. Considerable efforts were made to bring members of the community together in a meeting that was scheduled one evening. Unfortunately, the attendance was poor. The Anglos did not show up, and the project, for all practical purposes, came to an end. What happened? It is hard to know exactly, but these were my conclusions: There was no tradition for both groups to come together; distrust between the two groups was high; apathy by the two groups did not help; and Anglos felt that they had little, if anything, to gain.

The second initiative by the college was to create a new civic organization, the Junior Chamber of Commerce (Jaycees), in the Beeville community in hopes that there would be some cooperation between the younger business members of the community. The dean of the college invited a group of leaders from Corpus Christi to initiate this project. A group of Anglo Jaycees showed up with a lot of enthusiasm and support to help get the organization going. The dean quickly removed himself from the leadership position and passed it on to me. I became the president of the Jaycees. Several Anglo professors from the college and three Anglo members from the naval base became actively engaged with the organization. There was not a single Anglo member from the business community. We tried for a year, but without the backing of the business sector in the community, we could not get anywhere. Practically every business in town was owned by Anglos who had no desire to participate. We let the project die. Meanwhile, returning to the University of Oklahoma was far more important to me, although obtaining a doctoral degree was still a dream.

I was under constant watch by the president and certain faculty members. My personality, demeanor, and diplomacy were nonthreatening, but that was not enough. Threats, innuendos, and distrust were consistently present. Over time it came to a boiling point. The president started visiting my classes without asking for permission. His justification was that he had been a Texas legislator once and his interest in politics brought him there. Interestingly, he did not do this to anyone else. I tried to engage him in conversation with the students. This strategy put the students more at ease while I wondered how long this was going to last. It went on for about a semester, off and on. There was no question that these were acts of intimidation. He was looking for ways to get rid of me.

These were some of the misfortunes that occurred in a politically charged atmosphere. The president was uncomfortable, and he found avenues to demonstrate his dislike of my activities at the college. In the process the president called me for a meeting. He said, "Robert, I know that you have wanted to go back to the university to finish your degree, and I think that I can help you. I am planning to introduce a new policy to the Board for teaching enhancement—namely, a year's sabbatical leave at half of a professor's salary to continue your education, and you will be the first candidate." I told him that I welcomed the opportunity. Why did he want me to return to the university? I knew all along that he wanted me gone; that was why he made the offer. I took it. By the end of my first semester at the university, I had another call from the president. He said that he could extend the sabbatical for another year. This gave me the chance to finish all my course work and the comprehensive exam. I only had the dissertation left to write.

Since the day that I bought the new house, I knew that my return to the university was not going to be an easy task. We put the house on the market, and to our surprise, it sold without much difficulty. My wife immediately started to accumulate clothes for the children for a year since my salary was going to be cut in half. By the time we left for Oklahoma, Norma had done a tremendous job of consolidating our limited resources, and we were ready for a new adventure. I knew that I was going to miss some of the excitement and political controversies at the college and in the community. This period at the college set me on track to be committed to *la causa justa* (a just cause). This commitment will survive as long as I live.

After a year (1966–1967), in my first attempt to be at the University of Oklahoma, I made a few major mistakes. To correct these mistakes upon my return for the second time, I had to do something different. First, I was going to find a way to be an insider (i.e., be close to the faculty and graduate students); second, I would apply for a teaching assistant position; and third, Norma and I were committed to stayed together as a family.

When I met Norma, she was a professional woman in a position of leadership at a clothing store in downtown San Antonio. She decided that while the kids were young, she was going to take care of them, and I would be the financial provider. When I became a full-time student, I was still the only provider of this household. It worked well.

In our second trip (1970) to the University of Oklahoma, two of my nephews drove a pickup truck with our belonging to the same apartment where I stayed back in the fall of 1966. After we settled in for good, Carlos and Hilario took our two boys to Oklahoma City to see the Cowboy Hall of Fame, among other activities. My young sons were impressed with their two older cousins. Norma's parents did the same. Since I was a student again and unable to provide for the family, my mother-in-law took care of our first child while Norma worked full-time. Our means of transportation at the University of Oklahoma were limited, and I could not afford a bike. My in-laws got hold of pieces of an old bike and made it work. It was my vehicle for several years while at the university. Norma was relentlessly supportive of my seemingly dubious endeavors. She has always given her life and all her power for the development of our family, and I am one of the beneficiaries.

Our stay at the University of Oklahoma (1970–1972) was productive. Norma and the kids engaged themselves in educational and sports activities. Bee County College extended my sabbatical with pay for the following year. Two years later (1972), I had finished my coursework, passed my comprehensive finals, and started to do preliminary work on my dissertation. Throughout our stay I was a teaching assistant, and for a year I taught upper-division courses at Fort Sill in Lawton, Oklahoma. Once I finish my coursework and my written comprehensive final, we move back to Beeville so I could work full-time and write my dissertation. Moving back to Beeville depended on family assistance. Hilario and Sylvia Chapa, his wife, and my father came in a pickup truck with a two-horse trailer. Once again, the family convened to provide support.

I chose a dissertation topic that I knew little about. The reason was that in order to not have to take another foreign language that was required I had to incorporate my native language, Spanish, in my dissertation. So I chose Mexican American politics. It became the wisest choice in my research. Little had been written on this subject, and, ultimately, it became the research theme of my professional life. This was the easy part. Then came all the intricacies of writing the dissertation. First, my research skills were limited; second, choosing a manageable topic came with uncertainty; third, I had no person to turn to for assistance or advice; and fourth, I had no parameters to focus on the research. These were a few of the many issues before me. Without knowing it, I was ready to make multiple mistakes. For example, in the development of my questionnaire, I covered multiple disciplines, including economics, sociology, psychology, politics, history, race, and gender. The questionnaire had 150 questions, and I planned to personally interview over 200 people. This in itself shows my ambition and lack of experience.

The questionnaire was randomly administered to over 230 people in Beeville. Each one was personally interviewed. Once the interviews were over, I started to tabulate the data. At the end of this journey, I used less than 10 percent of the acquired data to write the dissertation.

The draft of the dissertation was over 350 pages. It never occurred to me that I could write that much. I thought that I did not know enough words in the English language. The work took three years. I had doubts about going in the right direction and doing quality work. Fortunately, the chair of my committee came to Padre Island for a short vacation in the summer months of 1975, and he made a point of stopping at our house. He reviewed the manuscript and told me that with minor changes, the dissertation was ready to be defended. July 1975 was the date of the defense. What a boost to my efforts and ego! I spent every minute that I could in preparation. Come July, I gathered five typed copies of the dissertation, and my family and I drove in a 1955 Oldsmobile 98 that I had bought from a friend of mine.

As soon as we arrived at the hotel, I began to organize the materials and my thoughts. Meanwhile, the chair, Sam Kirkpatrick, called and asked if we could have lunch with them before the one thirty meeting. I was enormously tired, so I asked Norma if she and the kids would go to lunch with them so I could take a short nap before the meeting. Well, it was not a wise decision. I overslept and missed the appointment. I woke up around two fifteen, scared to death. Norma had the car. I had no choice but to grab the dissertation copies and run like mad in the middle of July all the way to the building. I got to Sam's office, and he gave me a warm smile. Two hours later I was defending the work that I had done.

Defending the dissertation was far easier than I expected. I overestimated the knowledge of the committee members and underestimated the knowledge that I had acquired. See, it was always the same problem: underestimating myself. I had really done my homework, and the committee was highly impressed. They found a few technical errors, and Kirkpatrick assisted me in finding a typist to make the corrections.

The rules and regulations of the university required that I had to give finished copies to different corresponding offices. Approval came from all the offices except the graduate dean. She questioned the coloration of the typing on the manuscript. Without even reading the document, she flipped through the pages and claimed that the typing was inconsistent and, therefore, unacceptable. To type 356 pages with notes and a bibliography was a daunting task during the time when computers were unknown. What was I going to do? She indicated, however, that if the dissertation committee approved the document with the "imperfections," she would give approval, but it had to be in writing. I called Sam, and he was ready to act. The committee met for the third time and approved the document. Sam prepared a letter, and I made the delivery. I was *libre* at last, *libre* at last!

I had promised Norma that I was going to get drunk when I terminated this research project. When it was all over, I went to a liquor store and bought a bottle of vodka. I had one drink and went to bed. The bottle remained with us for years. This long and arduous road had come to an end. Looking back, it was nine years of hard work and uncertainty before it came to completion. There were many challenges, many lonely days and nights trying to figure out a path, and many trials and tribulations. Against the odds I managed to obtain the degree. It was a journey in turbulent water. On July 25, 1975, I finally got my doctoral degree. I had many people to be thankful for since they committed themselves to helping me. Starting with my wife, my mother, my father, all my siblings, and Norma's parents and sister, and I will not leave out Uncle Gregorio; he was a special *tio*! It is lamentable that my mother was not alive to see this milestone since she had a great appreciation for education. My father never got tired of assisting with my mother's wishes and being a good father. Their hard work helped me to get where I wanted to be. To me this was unimaginable. I will be forever thankful for all they did to see their family succeed. *Mama y Papa los adoro como siempre y que en paz descansen!*

On our way back from the University of Oklahoma, I began to map out the next step, to apply to universities and publish my dissertation. Teaching and doing research on Latino politics was very appealing to me. I still had an obligation with Bee County College to remain there for two years.

To continue supporting my family, I needed a twelve-month job, and the only way to do this was to become an administrator. I wrote a letter to the community college president asking to be considered for an administrative position. Two weeks later Grady called me and offered me the chair of the Social Studies Department, replacing Dr. Gus Dunn. I accepted the position. Unfortunately, I lost Gus's friendship since he thought that I was after his job. I never saw Gus Dunn again.

I was chair of the department for several months when Grady called me again and asked me to visit with him. I had no idea what he was up to since I had been to that office so many times. The president told me that he had just fired the director of the Federal Programs at the college. He claimed that he was "radical and irresponsible." He offered me the directorship. The director they had hired was a decent man, but his politics were too liberal and revolutionary for Beeville and South Texas. As part of the Civil Rights Movement, his explosive ideas only created chaos and confusion. I was as "radical" as he was, but I tempered my reactions, and my background in local politics was more acceptable.

I completed my two-year stay, and I was ready to move on. On my older son's tenth birthday, I was driving to El Paso for an interview at the University of Texas at El Paso.

Chapter 8

Coming to the Border
A Political and Cultural Nirvana

My roots are centered in South Texas and northern Mexico. This is where I was born; this is where I grew up; this is the world where my parents lived. Although we traveled to various places, South Texas was everything to us. The chapters that you have read, for the most part, have the strong cultural flavor of South Texas. By accident and not by design, I came to El Paso for an interview in 1976. Culturally, El Paso was a paradise when compared with my early years. Historically, the people from this Southwestern community have allowed more space for cultural coexistence, and they have sustained it. There was no concerted effort to eliminate one culture or replace it with another. Both dominant cultures have coexisted well and for a long time. In South Texas the consistent presence of the South, a culture long dominated by slavery, put us in a major predicament of lasting cultural oppression directed toward Mexicans. We can still see some of these effects today.

Following graduation I started looking at universities for a position. The responses were limited. The few that responded to, I was not interested in. On the other hand, the positions that I attained were offered to me without asking. This was true in every job that I attained. The following are positions that were offered to me that I did not pursue: Pawnee Middle School, Bee County College, University of Texas–Pan American, the University of Texas at El Paso, the executive directorship of the International Consortium, and the University of Texas at San Antonio. I have no explanation for these manifestations.

In early July 1976, my wife and I were preparing to take our kids to the beach at Padre Island. While we were in the process of leaving, the phone rang. It was the chair of the Political Science Department at the University of Texas at El Paso. He immediately told me he had spoken to my father about getting my phone number. Tony Kruszewski asked me if I was interested in a tenure-track position. I did not know where he was coming from since I had not applied there.

Let me backtrack: four years before, as I was trying to finish my dissertation at the University of Oklahoma, the Political Science Department sent my résumé to various universities in hopes of finding a job. I got a response from New Mexico State University and was asked to come in for an interview. With considerable hesitation, I turned it down. I felt that if I took a full-time job, I would never finish my dissertation, and I could not allow that to happen. My résumé remained at the department at New Mexico State for four years. For whatever reason, Kruszewski visited the chairman of the department at New Mexico State, and he gave him my file. That is how he got in touch with me.

The conversation with Kruszewski was brief. Kruszewski was Polish, and I was having difficulty understanding his accent. Nevertheless, I got the message, and I told him that I would get back to him in a few days. During the short trip to the beach, Norma and I discussed the offering. We were both excited about the possibility of going to El Paso, not knowing much about the place. Upon our return I called Tony and told him that I would accept the interview at the University of Texas at El Paso.

A long drive put us in El Paso that evening with a quick stop in Ozona, Texas, to visit Norma's godparents. Upon our arrival Tony gave me the details of the interview. It appeared that I was going back to the United States–Mexico border, and that was most acceptable.

My first impressions of this old West Texas town were encouraging. I felt a sense of belonging; the appreciation of the Mexican culture was unique; and it had a strong aura of cosmopolitanism. I felt at home. Multiculturalism and multiracialism dominated the broad metropolitan areas of El Paso–Cd. Juarez, Mexico. I knew that we had come to the right place. That evening Norma and I took a small tour of the beautiful and unique campus, Bhutanese style with thick-walled adobe buildings. The walls truly reminded me of the house that Dad had in Mexico. Unlike summer days in South Texas, El Paso's humidity was low. What a relief! Culturally, the university reflects the community.

The first part of the interview was informal. The Kruszewskis, Tony and June, invited us to have dinner with them at their home. Being Polish, they had a lot in common with us. We spent a wonderful evening. Before the formal interview, I was warned that a group of Chicano activists wanted a local person for the position. The students were not well regarded by either the faculty or the administration. The vice president for Academic Affairs joined Kruszewski in discouraging me from visiting with them. I think the administration's fear was that the students would drive me away. I felt compelled to hear them out since I had cultural affinity with these folks. The meeting lasted an hour. There was nothing I could do to convince the students. I finally told them that their rejection put me on the hands of the Anglos, and so it did. It came down to the question of whether I would accept the position or not.

The folks at the University of Texas at El Paso kept a busy schedule. The interviews with the vice president, the dean, and the department were done swiftly, without a hitch, and the tour of the campus was delightful. Unquestionably, the meeting with the department was going to be rigorous. The chair of the department took me in and gave me some advice as to the characters of the department and various key players. I had a special warning about one of the older professors on campus, Dr. Melvin P. Straus. I was told that Mel was going to raise questions at the end of the interview and that some of his questions were hard to understand, much less to provide answers to. When I met with the members of the department at the end of the session, Mel raised his hand. "Here we go," I thought.

He welcomed me and thanked me as he started with his lengthy question. My thoughts were not necessarily to give Mel a proper answer but to at least sound intelligible. As he continued to construct his question, a thunderstorm struck with ferocity (it was monsoon season). In El Paso people are always thirsty for rain, so instead of following the end of Melvin's question, the faculty looked out the window and shouted, "It's raining!" Poor Mel was drowned out with the noise. I understood his question, though, and I gave it a shot. Straus became one of my most trusted friends on campus, a selfless man with great devotion to the community and the university.

As the interviews continued, I found myself being wanted, and it was encouraging. I felt that I was in the right place at the right time. One evening my wife and I were taken to dinner at one of the swankiest places in El Paso. Red carpet treatment continued to be new to me, although I faced a somewhat similar situation when I had arrived in Beeville back in 1967. It was, indeed, the politics of tokenism, an attempt by the institution to emphasize one person of different origin—in this case, Mexican. I contend that this was not about me or my great qualifications. They were looking for good symbol to face the community, and I was that person.

By the time we left El Paso, I had signed a contract. I became a tenure-track assistant professor of political science. I did not know exactly what tenure-track meant. After signing my contract with the university, we returned home to begin the process of moving. This was July, and we had to move by August. Days after we arrived home, I had a call from Dr. Jerry Polinard, chair of the Political Science Department at Pan American University. I knew Jerry; we had been friends for a while. Jerry's call was to offer a position available in his department. Without delay I told Jerry that I had signed a contract with the University of Texas at El Paso. The contract did not dissuade Jerry. Instead, he wanted me to bring the whole family with me. I went for the interview.

The interview went well, and at the end I was offered a contract. Now I had two contracts, and I had a month to sell the house, move the whole family, and prepare for classes. But this was not the end of possible offers. I got a call from my alma mater, Texas A&I University, requesting an interview. Graciously, I turned them down. I became convinced that the University of Texas at El Paso was a far more mature place to conduct research. Still, Jerry offered a better salary than El Paso. I thought about it, then I called Tony Kruszewski and gave him the news. He understood, and he told me that he would inquire about the request to increase my salary. A day later I got a call from Dr. Rudy Gomez, the graduate dean and a professor of political science. He said that the university was willing to match the amount Jerry offered; however, as far as Pan American being closer to my family, there was nothing that he could do. I called Jerry and thanked him for the opportunity. We were looking west, and west we went!

By the end of the fall semester, we had bought a house, and during spring break we moved the rest of the furniture. We landed in west El Paso, where most of the political science faculty lived. We remained there for almost thirty years. My colleagues were very helpful and made us feel at home. This was the beginning of an entirely different experience, and for the first time in my professional life, I was among equals. I could not ask for more. Now it was time to prove my maturity, professional skills, and leadership. I felt enthusiastic and ready.

Living in an international and cosmopolitan city adjacent to a major sister city (Cd. Juarez) and working at an emerging university that was growing at a fast pace (and was a Hispanic-serving institution) created an ambience of growth and participation. Recently, the University of Texas at El Paso's research status and growth were magnified by the Carnegie Classification of Higher Education Institutions designation as one of the nation's top-tier research universities. This is an honor of distinction, as "UTEP stands among a group of 187 R1 universities out of nearly 4,000 accredited degree-granting institutions nationwide, placing it in the top 5% for research productivity. The University is also one of only 19 Hispanic-Serving Institutions to achieve this prestigious classification."[1] The evolving growth of Latino students and the evolution of graduate degrees made El Paso a powerful place to offer services.

El Paso and the university are at the crossroads between Los Angeles, California, and Austin and San Antonio, Texas. This made a significant difference in the culture and politics of the community, with practically no influence from the Southern states. By any measure, El Paso is underestimated, underrated, underappreciated, and undervalued. Nationally, the city is perceived as being poor. Migration coming across the border makes the city unattractive to Anglos, and it is perceived as being lesser. It does not fit the stereotype of a great American city. This sense of prejudice and ignorance predominates, and it has expanded, as is well exemplified by President Trump and all his surrogates, including the Republican Party. All these negatives can turn into positives when you live there and know the place. The culture and people of El Paso are unique. There are no significant barriers between ethnic and racial groups. Violence in this border town is less than many other places across the state and country. Politically, there is no dominant group. I could not be prouder of being part of this border community. The culture gave me warmth, a feeling I had never experienced before, by any ideology.

The university reflects the cultural environment of the community. The Bhutanese adobe architecture of the university has all the qualities of houses in northern Mexico and southern New Mexico. The style of the buildings brought up some memories of my childhood when I used to go to Mexico to visit our relatives where my parents were born. Benedict Hall, home of the Department of Political Science, is one of the older buildings, located almost at the center of the university. I felt right at home.

A manifestation of this institution was the fluidity and common acceptance of ethnic expressions and identity compared to South Texas. The value given to the Mexican culture is far more appreciated by Anglos in El Paso than it is in South Texas, although they would never publicly or politically admit it. As it can be common for people who have lived in a place for a long time, the Latino community takes its rich culture for granted. I came from a different world, like most of my colleagues that I interviewed in the survey. I had greater appreciation than some of the natives. I was ready to integrate into the richness of this culture since South Texas denied our culture and heritage, particularly in the early years of my life. El Paso was a sound base to learn and mature, and mature I did.

The center of my work and political activities was the Department of Political Science. The heart of departmental activities can make or break you. There were many cases in my department, as well as others, in which a faculty member would join the institution but, for various reasons, would not thrive. When I joined the department faculty in 1976, there were four new tenure-track professors who came to campus. Two were pushed out in a matter of a year, and the third left to teach at an out-of-state university. In a matter of two years, I was the only one left from that group.

Based on the policies of the institution, my job had three main components: teaching, research, and serving the university and community. These three major activities do not mention "politics." Still, just about everything that moves in any organization requires politics. It is necessary to keep your ear to the ground and be attentive. So the life of a professor is complicated by the politics of the department and the university. I knew early in the game that if I was going to lead, I had to play hardball, be tactful, and truly pay my dues. Being the only Latino in the department, I was held to a different standard, tinged with curiosity, suspicion, and animosity. Fortunately, I have never been paranoid. Yet in the early stages of my career, the political culture of higher education was new to me. I had to learn quickly. Chicano faculty were under pressure since we represented the community better: a whopping 87 percent of the El Paso population was Hispanic and the majority of the student body was Hispanic. Yet the representation of Chicano faculty was miniscule. Gender, ethnicity, and the overlapping of two dominant cultures at an international border setting is a prime justification for a vastly complex system. To counterbalance this profound situation, I had to calibrate my every move and make connections peacefully. I was fortunate to have the patience and understanding to appreciate this environment. From that perspective, I came to the university with open-minded experience. In my childhood living in two worlds, I gained the tools to navigate between two culturally distinct groups and to have the ability to work, accept, and be part of both. In my early years I had a model for diplomacy (my mother). This gave me the strength to succeed. Yet when the time came for me to pursue the possibility of being the chairman of the department, there was opposition from some faculty members. One of the most influential members of the department claimed that I was "too Hispanic" to represent and be chair of the department.

Teaching has a lot of components besides lecturing and holding seminars. I was constantly involved in committee work and continuously asked to supervise student research papers, public administration capstones, theses, and dissertation committees. These are most rewarding experiences, but they are enormously time consuming. To a lot of graduate students, I was known as a good guy. Although this is appreciated, it certainly carried extra loads of work. Based on the criteria of the university, our most important work was to teach students, and we did. But most universities want to excel and be known, and teaching is not the way to get there. In order to be recognized, research, acquiring grants, writing, and publications are at the heart of a university. Based on this reality, I set out to do research, publish, and get tenure, never leaving teaching behind.

Despite difficulties, including mental illness, I never yielded. I faced them head-on. I never turned down a speaking engagement.

It was agony when I was asked to speak since I was tormented prior to the presentation. Given the situation, I still had the courage, desire, and *orgullo* (pride) to offer my services no matter what happened. Somehow, I felt that if I caved in, it would become worse. The same was true in the classroom; I never failed to make a presentation before the students. It was my job, and I always carried it out to the letter.

One day, by accident, I met a colleague from the Psychology Department. Guido Barrientos, Columbian born, had been part of the university for years. This was the first time I was able to talk to someone besides my wife about my sickness. He told me that he had an office downtown where he treated people for various illnesses and suggested I visit him on Saturdays. He knew I had insurance, but he immediately said that he did not want to talk about that. He wanted to help me as a colleague. He emphasized that he wanted to pay me back for what I had done for the Latino and university communities.

For almost a year I visited him at his office. We got to know each other well and became good friends. We did a series of psychological exercises. Some were awfully painful. Along those lines, we also discussed the current issues that we were facing at the university. Gradually, I started to become myself again. Over time I became free from these fears and anxieties. I am indebted to Guido for his expertise and loyalty. Guido died recently, and it is sad to say that I have two books from his collection that I never returned to him. Rest in peace, my good friend. What I learned from this terrible experience was to stop looking up to people thinking that they were better than I was. It is sad that you learn to be submissive and never look at someone as being equal. Dr. Barrientos took care of that; I am now free to look at people for what they are, eye to eye.

To gain stability and be recognized at a university, it is necessary to become tenured. To become tenured, it takes six years of hard work. At the end of this period, a decision is made about whether you stay or not. The purpose of tenure is to provide the opportunity for a professor to speak the truth on issues without the threat of being fired. Being in the world of politics, I took the issue seriously. Politics can be extremely controversial. As to the idea of keeping a job for the rest of my life, it was not a concern of mine.

Tenure and promotion come with a lot of work and responsibility. Teaching and research are only part of the work. The university was organized by committees for every category, and I was expected to participate at all levels of the institution, including as a faculty advisor to the Texas University System for a number of years. All these committees are recommending bodies without much power. Even more demanding were the departmental committees for library, executive, budget, student affairs, and academics. For the most part, faculties serve only the department and college committees. I embraced the entire spectrum of the university system. It was a whole lot of work and responsibility, but it was also enjoyable since I was often surrounded by great people, including community leaders, staff, and other faculty. A small tour of my curriculum vitae denotes these undertakings. The reward of this work for tenure was limited at best. I knew this, but I felt that it was important to be exposed to other venues and ideas. I worked together with other colleagues as the president of the Graduate Council for four years. This was a policy-recommending body on curriculum matters.

The 1970s and 1980s were most productive for Latinos at the university. One of the great joys of being in El Paso was working with the communities of El Paso and Cd. Juarez. I deeply loved and respected how these old communities worked and established themselves. They have a strong cultural affinity and have been most adaptable for people who come from outside. I was one of them.

Knowing little about the El Paso–Cd. Juarez community, it did not take me long before I became integrated into the ways of life, aspirations, and needs of the community. The community was friendly to everyone, particularly to Chicanos, and welcomed people from the university, especially when very few faculty members participated in community affairs. This gave me the opportunity to help people of Mexican origin do better. This was a commitment that I made to myself for my parents, that I would do everything possible in their name. Like many people of Mexican origin, they contributed greatly to this nation without recognition or reward. From this perspective, I responded through political activism. It is through political activism that we can bring greater justice and equality. I joined the Hispanic leaders of the community. I also joined other groups seeking greater participation in the university and used my expertise in the science of politics.

The impact of the Civil Rights Movement proved to be stimulating to a dormant Latino community. Chicanos at the university were the catalyst for demonstrations, including taking over the Office of Academic Affairs as UTEP. Chicano leaders were determined to bring change and to awaken the community to a better world that could be found by fighting for the right causes. Although not much change occurred from this development, it made a great contribution to opening doors for more moderate groups to raise the banner and move forward with new organizations. The passing of this movement created a breath of fresh air that called for new organizational initiatives to cope with the many needs of the Hispanic community. It created a fertile land to create new organized efforts to resolve a sundry of issues. In a matter of a few years, we cofounded several organizations that continue to operate today, including the Hispanic Leadership Institute and the El Paso del Norte Public Policy Institute, which was created by two educational institutions: El Paso Community College and the University of Texas at El Paso. I served as one of the principal leaders of these organizations.

At the university there was a division between Anglos and Latinos. But the division came from small groups of extremists from both sides. As may be expected, the university was far more anglicized than the community of El Paso. On the other hand, the community always looked up to its only university. The big reason that I was well accepted by Latino community leaders was that I was coming and representing the university and, no question, the Latino leadership had open arms to bring people from the university to be part of them.

The politics of ethnicity seemed to be present in practically every aspect of life. When I was appointed director of the Chicano Studies Center at the university, some members of the Chicano faculty and staff were concerned that I was not Chicano enough. The general distrust among some of them was based mainly on ideological grounds. Throughout the struggle of the Chicano movement, I always sought moderation and pragmatism. Although most of us had the same goals, our ways of getting there were different. Thinking that radical activities had passed their time, I tried to temper my actions with practicality and realization in terms of what could be achieved. But I had a narrow path to walk. The political environment of the university community involved two elements: We were under the watchful eye of the Anglo community, and Chicanos struggled with themselves. Sometimes, there was little in-between or ways to compromise. As a director I tried to move to the political center to accommodate the wishes of the university and attract more politically moderate support. I created and organized a variety of activities to give visibility to the program and invite elements of the university community to participate. I spent considerable time with some faculty members who believed in the movement but were alienated by the radicals on campus. These were more moderate Chicanos. Over time, the center of the movement became more acceptable to the university, the faculty, and the community. Trust was developed among the base group, and life continued.

With the cooperation of the vice president for Academic Affairs, we started an hour-long program on the local public radio station, KTEP, on Hispanic issues that pertained to the community and the university. Over time, the program became popular. A nationally known poet, Pat Mora, astutely crafted the program to serve the community by inviting influential members from the university and the community to speak on various topics. In our efforts to promote the presence and importance of Latinos on campus, a group of us started meeting at Jalisco, a local restaurant in the Segundo Barrio in south El Paso. The Jalisco group was composed of approximately eight leaders from the university who met to plan and expand our activities on campus. As part of our work, we requested the creation of an advisory group to work directly with the vice president of the university, Joe Olander. He accepted the challenge, and Pat Mora became the chair of the group. Although Joe was sympathetic with our intentions, he had little room to operate and not a lot of power. One of the problems in dealing with him was the way he conducted himself with some people and students. He acquired a bad reputation among administrators and faculty. Let me cite an example: Joe started dating a freshman student. One time he came to my office to see if I had a book for her since she was taking a basic course in American government. This, indeed, was considered a social scandal.

With Olander we made few gains, though the organized efforts served well to air out our frustrations. One fateful day we scheduled a meeting with him. We met and waited for him to arrive so we could start the meeting. He walked in and it was immediately obvious that he was in trouble. The first thing he said was, "You know I cannot trust you! You did me in! Here I am trying to help your situation, and you turn around and stab me."

I asked myself, what have we done? I was stunned like everyone else. After a moment of silence, I asked him to tell us what we had done wrong. We could not think of anything that we had done since we were relatively powerless, and we never communicated with other administrators on campus. In this immediate ordeal, I kept thinking that all our efforts were going down the drain. Another moment of silence passed that felt like years. We were in the vice president's conference room. After much silence, Olander got up, walked toward me, and gave me a kiss on top of my bald head. I was stunned again. He went back to his chair and said, "I am sorry. I am angry and disappointed, but it has nothing to do with all of you. Let us move to the agenda of the day." The meeting concluded, and we continued to be confused and dumbfounded.

Prior to this meeting I planned a gathering at home and invited Pat Mora, his assistant, to recite new poems with some of our colleagues.

In the middle of her presentation, the doorbell rang, and it was Joe Olander. He came to let us know that he had just been fired. It was a sad evening. We never formally met again with him, and Joe Olander left town, never to be seen again. Once again, the doors of the university were closed to us.

Notwithstanding these challenges, the group kept meeting to develop momentum and try new ideas. At one point we decided to have a get-together once every year during the early fall semester for a Dies y Seis de Septiembre celebration at my house and invite all the university's influential movers and shakers, including the president, top administrators, and faculty. By that time we had some influence, and everybody who was invited came. The focus of the gathering was the lack of university's accountability toward Hispanics. The program was moderated by Pat Mora and highlighted the year's successes and failures regarding the promotions and tenures of Chicano faculty. In subtle and not-so-subtle ways, we tried to pressure the administration to do better over time for the Hispanics on campus. The gathering was in the backyard of my house. The program was well prepared and well administered. There were food, drinks, and entertainment. Ultimately, the administration provided funds for this event. The message was simple: The administration was not doing enough to correct the long-time problem of underserving Hispanics. It took several years, but we made gains in increasing the number of Latino faculty, administrators, and some top staff members.

As director of the Chicano Studies Program, in conjunction with many faculty members, we worked to create a research center where we could acquire grants and publish scholarly materials. Support from the administration was not there since the origins of the program were strictly for curriculum matters, and that was used as an excuse to not take it further. Moreover, from an administrative perspective, the program had a distasteful background since *Chicanismo* was a bad word, and Anglos were fearful. My focus was to repair this situation. I proceeded to start a series of publications, and I invited scholars from throughout the Southwest to submit manuscripts. The response was considerable. A lot of Latino scholars were looking for outlets to publish since mainstream publishers refused to publish their books and articles. Knowing this reality, I became convinced that scholarly publications would give us greater visibility and attention. I created an editorial board composed of established scholars from the university who were sensitive to Latino issues. The board members covered a wide spectrum of academic disciplines, and some Anglos were part of the board. For several years the board worked diligently on research topics not published elsewhere. Although we felt we had accomplished some things, it was not enough. We had limited resources, and the university was not willing to commit itself to these and other endeavors.

To create greater visibility and community participation, the Chicano Studies Program sponsored a speaker series through which presentations could be edited and published. With top scholars making presentations, we had good and steady attendance, not only from the university but also from the community. The presentations covered a variety of topics from different disciplines. At one of our events, Manuel Pacheco, prior to becoming president of the University of Arizona, was on campus for two years, so we knew him well. This and many other activities that I have outlined were major parts of convincing the university and community that our involvement was important and critical to the university and community. Yet in the minds of the president and other administrators, they saw Chicano Studies as a program not in line with the whole agenda of the university.

The culmination of six years of being the director of the center came when I decided to invite the National Association of Chicano Studies to have its annual national conference at the university. This organization that continues to exist represents the world of *Chicanismo* throughout the Southwest and other parts of the nation. It took a lot of doing to get this together. My wife and I traveled to Sacramento, California, to the association's national conference, in an attempt to persuade the leadership that El Paso was the epicenter of Chicanos in the United States and northern Mexico. We were competing against three other universities. When it came down to budgets to finance the conference, we were short of funds compared with the other three groups. In fact, we had no budget. But being from El Paso made a world of difference to the members of the organization. Without much discussion the leaders of the conference voted to have the meeting in El Paso the following year. My dilemma was how to finance the conference since the university officials were not enthusiastic about the idea. We needed a minimum of $20,000. It was a mystery to us where the money was going to come from.

To organize the coming conference, I created a steering committee composed of Latino leaders from across campus. By any standards, the members of the steering committee were heavyweights. The group was talented and dedicated. It became one of the most enlightened groups I have ever worked with. I worked closely with the vice president for Academic Affairs while I created an auxiliary staff to do the groundwork. It was the best staff one could ever have. They were loyal, bright, committed, cooperative, and mature. It was an enormous pleasure to work with them. We had all the talent that was necessary to put together a first-class conference, and we did. However, the money to glue this together was not there. In the process, however, the vice president became convinced that it was an asset to the university.

A retired Army colonel, well-known and respected in the community, was my next target. He was a former graduate student of mine. I visited him and told him about the financial dilemma of the conference. Colonel Raul Garibay positively responded to the challenge. In order to accomplish the assigned task, he asked to have another graduate student to help him. They went to work right away. For ideological reasons I decided to keep him separate from the other two committees that I had organized. I told both committees when we met that I had someone who had volunteered to raise the funds. I had full trust in the colonel and from the committees. In a matter of a month, he had raised over $15,000.

This work was internal, and I had some control. The only resistance we faced was from a former director of this program, Ricardo

Aguilar. I knew Ricardo well since we had worked together on many occasions. I soon learned that he was actively communicating with several leaders from the National Association of Chicano Studies, and his commentary was negative. I never knew the cause of Aguilar's actions. We proceeded to implement the scope of this large conference. More than two hundred Chicano scholars attended and participated in the conference. We even invited scholars from la Universidad Autonoma de Cd. Juarez to participate, and they did. One evening during the conference, we went to Cd. Juarez, Mexico, where several Mexican scholars made presentations. It was an absolute triumph!

As a faculty member, I also served as an administrator for most of my career. In various administrative positions I averaged around six years per position. I found it unhealthy to serve longer. At the end of my sixth year as director of Chicano Studies, I decided that it was time to move on. Later, I learned from one of my colleagues that the chair of the department was completing the maximum amount of time allowed, and that there was going to be an opening the coming fall semester. Melvin Straus, my perennial colleague, offered to assist. I found this offer most attractive since no person of Mexican origin had ever served as chair. Once again, it was time to break another barrier.

From time to time, Straus would communicate with me on the status of the election. A key player in the department was Richard Bath, who felt that I was too involved with Hispanic affairs and not prepared to do the administrative work for the department as chair. The reality was that there were two other candidates interested in the position. Mel, an astute politician, worked closely with every member of the department in hopes of getting a majority vote. When it came down to the last lap, there was one colleague in doubt whom we needed in order to make it to a majority vote. So when we went to the meeting, I had no assurance of winning. The chair of the meeting called for nominations, and Straus nominated me for the position. Someone seconded the nomination. There was a moment of silence. Somebody else moved to close the nominations and asked for unanimous consent, and the meeting was over. I became the first Chicano chair of the Department of Political Science. I was relieved; I thanked everyone, and I told them that I would do my best to represent them in the best way possible.

I proceeded to serve the department without interruption. It was the most difficult job I had. There were considerable responsibilities and limited power to act. Having the departmental faculty constantly nearby can be troublesome. Before the end of the second term, I was appointed as vice president for Academic Affairs, and I was relieved from my administrative duties in the department. I served for six years in this position. When I returned to the department, the same person who claimed that I was too Hispanic to be chair of the department came to my office and asked me if I would serve again. Richard Bath told me that he was planning to retire, and he wanted me to handle the paperwork appropriately. He did his homework, and I was elected for the third time. Soon after, my colleague retired.

The vice presidency was a whole new ball of wax. Instead of being confined to one department, the spectrum changed to a world unknown to me. Like in my professional past, I learned quickly. The range and volume of work were phenomenal and exciting, from firing the director of the library to defending the university at a federal trial; from settling personnel disputes and being the main speaker at conferences on campus to working closely with the University of Texas system and interviewing and hiring new personnel. Once again, it was a first for the university to have a Hispanic in this position, and it was a first for me. It was a great honor!

After serving as director of Chicano Studies, chair of the Department of Political Science, and vice president of Academic Affairs, I decided to run for president of the Graduate Council, a recommending body on major policy issues regarding curricula. This position was elected by the entire graduate faculty. Being appointed to a position is radically different than being elected. Yet in all cases, I was subtle, quiet, and worked hard not to disturb the peace and politics to the best of my abilities. Competing against two other candidates, I was elected as chair of the organization for a two-year term. I ran for the second time and won again. This two-term position was intense, and I always sought the cooperation of the faculty and the administration. Once again, I was the first Mexican American to be president of the Graduate Council.

Throughout the years that I spent at the university, one aspect of service to the community was interviews with the press, television, and local, national, and international groups. News coming over the wire covered a wide range of political topics and places: from *The New York Times* to *The El Paso Times* and from KTSM to CNN. The topics ranged from the politics of the Soviet Union to why some Hispanics would put their small savings under their mattresses instead of in banks.

After close to thirty years in El Paso, my wife and I decided that it was time to go back home. To us El Paso was a paradise unknown, a home away from home. But family is far more important. Our parents, uncles, aunts, cousins, brothers, and sisters needed our presence and attention. Some of them were getting old—too old. Knowing the circumstances of our family in South Texas, it was not a hard decision to come home. We loved El Paso, and our lengthy stay was magnificent, but there is an end to every story. As we were transitioning from El Paso to the San Antonio area, my brother Epifanio Jr. died in Florida. My wife and I attended the funeral in Tampa. Norma's mother also passed on after we got here. Soon after, my sister Minerva died, too. Not long after Minerva died, my brother Gonzalo died. With no intent to be melancholic, these are some of the realities of life. At the prime of my professional life, I resigned my tenure position, so I was able to move closer to our family back in South Texas. To some of my colleagues, this action was beyond their comprehension. To me it was not a difficult decision since family comes first. Norma and I were convinced that we made the right decision.

When I retired from the University of Texas at El Paso, I was offered a job as executive director of the International Consortium for Health and Environmental Security at Brooks Air Force Base in San Antonio. It was an ambitious project that involved a team of approximately thirty research scientists from various universities whose job was to study the migration of various diseases. This was a collaborative effort with the Center of Epidemiology at Brooks Air Force Base. I had the opportunity to work with them and several health and environmental authorities from northern Mexico. The change from a university atmosphere to directing an international consortium on health and the environment was drastic. Now I am not tenured; I am all by myself visiting strangers in hope that they would support and contribute to the development of the consortium; I am driving all over the United States–Mexico border and connecting with interested Mexican organizations that share our work. My outlook of the world changed. But in a short period of time, I learned new skills to survive and thrive. Like most administrative jobs, politics was the name of the game. I was fortunate to have a lot of experience.

Epilogue

Yo Soy is a multigenerational epic that takes eight chapters to cover a story of generations. Somewhere, somehow, younger and future generations need to know and understand the background of our educational institutions in Texas. My life paralleled with the historical surroundings that I grew up in and my struggles to grow out of the confines of this environment to be a productive citizen. This development took generations and many people with a commitment to change, starting with my family and moving on to a multiplicity of components as I navigated many roads in hopes of reaching my destination. The main focus of this fight has been to gain greater social justice and equality. As a child I chose the formal education route. Based on this background and with the assistance of many others, I have tried to make an evaluation of what transacted during this time. These transactions and relations between Anglos and Latinos took years for each to better understand the other. To have a better understanding of the results, integration between the two dominant groups is a better way of measuring changes. Anything worthwhile takes time, and these two ethnic groups have been side by side for more than two hundred years.

Unlike Canada, Mexico has never been a favorite nation of the United States or its people. Although we enjoy the products of Mexico, the beauty of this country, and all the pleasantries for vacations, we do not appreciate Mexico itself. The exploitation of Mexican labor has been well documented; discrimination against Mexicans has been rampant; and anti-Mexican violence in Texas continues along the US-Mexico border.

Notwithstanding a long history of hostility and suppression, the Latino community has been vibrant and a great contributor to nation building. They have been involved in every aspect of making the United States into what it is and have constructively participated in modes of production, politics, social relations, and cultural understanding. Today, Mexican Americans contribute more than ever to this nation.

The evolution of these two groups has brought us to a greater level of justice and equality. Now, cooperation and integration seem to work far better than in the past. In some ways, it should be understood that coming together is inevitable. That being said, what follows is a qualitative assessment of how the two dominant groups are coalescing with each other and providing greater integration. For years the relations between the two groups were characterized by a language of separation: "them" and "us." This was based on a world of one group dominating the other. This has changed for the better. Unquestionably, the social, economic, and political barriers still exist, but these barriers are coming down. Now in any relationship, Latinos cannot be taken for granted, not like they used to be.

For years Anglos voted during elections and we did not. Since voting is a middle-class activity, voting in my family was not an issue, and I can speak for the entire Latino community where I lived. There were no guilty feelings, it was just a matter of fact.

In 1948 my father bought an eighty-acre piece of land in northern Bee County at a time when few Mexican Americans owned land. The first oil well in Bee County was on Dad's eighty acres. Our social status changed. Epifanio became Mr. Villarreal. My father worked and collaborated with many Anglos on equal footing. Now, both groups diligently participate in the political process, and the participation of Latinos is a reality. Elective participation of Latinos is still not up to par with Anglos, but it is forthcoming.

The expansion of education and the rise of the middle-class among Hispanics has changed these relations. Anglos and Hispanics have come closer to harmony and equality. Nothing has been more important than formal education for the rise of minorities. A count of elementary, middle, and high schools' Latino students and graduation rates demonstrate what the future holds for these two groups. These changes will provide greater production and competition, and they will impact the culture of the entire school system, manifesting greater affluence for the Latino community as their voices are rising to claim what is right for them.

Anglos have a greater need to associate with and depend on Latinos more than ever before. This is part of their survival. Like yesteryear, Anglos for the most part are subtle and quiet on race and ethnic issues. Yet many are searching to find a path for greater integration that would work to their advantage. Anglos are slowly learning to appreciate who we are, including a better understanding of the underpinnings of the Mexican culture. It is understood that these changes did not happen by accident. It took years of hard work to make it happen, and public education has been an uplifting factor. It is a slow process, but the growth of the middle-class and formal education have led to greater assimilation and acculturation. The bulk of this population affirms the ethos of American society. Interestingly, as Mexican Americans have gained more power and prestige, they are regaining greater pride of their ancestries. The pride of the Latino culture and heritage have and will impact the Anglo community.

In terms of integration, let me compare the past with the present. In prior chapters I wrote on my experiences in the public schools, where social and ethnic distances were well defined. For example, in the spring semester of my senior year in high school, two of my classmates, Mary Ann and Irene (both Anglos), were seeking transportation to get things for the high school senior prom. I offered to take them and bring them back to their houses. It never occurred to me that I had crossed a social-ethnic line. When we arrived at Mary Ann's house, her father came out to talk to me. Marry Ann got out and went inside, and I was left to deal with him. Her father asked me what I was doing with his daughter and told me, clearly, "We belong to a different group, and you are only causing trouble. You are getting my family in trouble, and you are getting your parents in trouble too." I tried to respond; he did not want to listen. I never told my parents about this incident. These types of social interactions were common between the two ethnic groups then, but not anymore.

These ethnic divisions occurred when I was in college. At that time Anglo men could date Mexican American women but Mexican American men could do not date Anglo women, especially if they were from South Texas. I dated an Anglo woman from Houston, and at one social event that we attended, a close friend and his date were shocked to see me with an Anglo woman. This was considered a rarity. As time went on, things began to change, and the door began to open for more integration, though perhaps short of marriage. When we returned to South Texas in the early twenty-first century, an increase in social integration was taking place. Social relations have continued to improve, and intermarriages are becoming common. My family exemplifies the community. Several of my nephews and nieces are married to Anglos; I have three children, and two have married Anglo girls (one is Jewish). This kind of intimate relationship is growing, and there are no boundaries. Integration is occurring practically everywhere, in all aspects of life. However, two distinctions should be made when considering these ethnic groups. Socially, integration is occurring rapidly. But wealth between the two groups is another matter. When we consider money-earning jobs, the two groups are competitive. But when we evaluate the ownership of land and natural resources underneath, there is a considerable difference. Among Anglos, old money and land keep moving from one generation to another. There is no old money or land on the part of Mexican Americans.

Historically, this lack of social integration has come from both groups. In a survey that I conducted in Beeville, Texas, as part of my doctoral dissertation back in the 1970s, I tried to measure social distance between Mexican Americans and Anglos and between Mexican Americans and Blacks. The sample involved 230 people. The responses were as follows:

Mexican Americans found it distasteful to

Eat with Anglos	10%
Dance with Anglos	23%
Party with Anglos	41%
Marry Anglos	23%

Then, the same questions were asked to Mexican Americans about Blacks.

It was deemed distasteful to

Eat with Blacks	21%
Dance with Blacks	55%
Party with Blacks	50%
Marry Blacks	80%

Based on this and other studies, the Mexican American community consistently looks up to Anglos, largely because of their wealth, status, and skin color. If I were to conduct this survey today, it would not have the same results. There is greater closeness. Today, the Black population in Beeville is also closer to Mexican Americans and to Anglos.

The concept of the *vendido* (turncoat—members of a minority group siding and defending Anglos against their own group) played a significant role in generations past. The Mexican American community suffered from this phenomenon. It was an enigma. Simply put, it was hell if you did and hell if you didn't in terms of getting close to or distancing from whites. If a Mexican American became close to the Anglos, and many did, members of our community would be overly critical to the point of ostracizing those individuals. When I came to Beeville in the late 1960s as the only professor of Mexican origin at Bee County College, the Mexican Americans in the community were starting to politically organize as a way to defend themselves. Accordingly, the Anglos were prepared to respond. Since the community placed great value on the educational institution and I was the only Latino faculty member, I automatically became one of the leaders. Under those circumstances, it was easy to be considered a *vendido*. I tried my best to stay neutral, but it was almost impossible. I was pulled by both sides, and I was welcomed by both sides. Today, this issue has subsided and Latinos occupy greater political influence. The concept of the turncoat has practically been left behind, providing the opportunity for both groups to come closer together.

Another aspect of integration is the generational difference between younger and older Anglos and younger and older Latinos. Past generations from the twentieth century are different from current generations. We live in a world where changes are occurring far faster than ever before. The increase of the middle class among the Latino population has had a considerable impact. The growth and education of this group has been an important factor toward the integration. The increase in the occupational levels of Mexican Americans in respected occupations has given them greater power and visibility. Let us consider public schools. In practically every school in South Texas, the majority of students are Mexican Americans. There is also an increase in those serving as staff, faculty, and administrators. The number of school board members are also increasing. Meanwhile, Anglo educators continue to yield to pressure. This revolution is conducive to integration.

In my generation (1940s to 1960s), the intermarriage of Mexican Americans with Anglos was out of the question. If a person was from another part of the country, there was a possibility of marital relations. During my public-school years, I am certain that some Anglo students had preferences for Mexican American students, but if the preferences were there, they were not known. I had a similar experience when I was in elementary school. There was an Anglo girl who cared for me, and I felt the same way. That was it. It was well understood that there would be no open relations whatsoever. So we remained in that state until we departed from school. When I joined the teaching profession soon after I married Norma, I faced a similar situation. As I grew older in my professional career, I had many opportunities to be in a relationship with an Anglo woman. I am not making assumptions; they declared themselves. As far as I know, they were respectful to my wife, but the notion was that if I were not married, they would want to marry me. Sometimes it was hard to resist, but I had to let them go. I remained married to Norma for sixty years. Those opportunities never came during my youth when I was single.

Historically, skin color has been a factor in integration between the two groups. Notwithstanding the efforts and rhetoric of the Latino population, showing pride and dignity of being mestizos was only part of the equation since the power and dominance of whiteness continues to be significant to most people. Is this racist? Is it bigotry? It does not seem to matter. It is consistent with the credo found in both the Latino and Anglo cultures. For Mexican Americans the appeal of whiteness prevails, and the preference for whiteness is truly alluring and enduring. For example, in Pawnee, where I went to high school, we have had school reunions every four years. In one of the reunions that I attended, one of my former classmates (an Anglo) saw me and with great delight he said, "Hi, Robert, you are white like us." At that point I was white. I could easily tell that for whatever reason, I was being welcomed, and I was with them.

My father was a prime example of this phenomenon. Epifanio was six-foot-four, *muy guero* (light complexion), with green eyes and curly hair. At that time we did not know that he was part Jewish. Dad took full advantage of these physical characteristics. When we lived in South Texas and in Northwest Texas, we were not allowed in Anglo restaurants, and at that time there were no Mexican restaurants. When we migrated to pick cotton in the panhandle of Texas, from time to time Dad would try to go to restaurants. My father would be admitted, but if Mom would come along, the picture would change. They would be asked to eat in the kitchen although they never did. Whiteness can be a significant factor for human beings. Time and socioeconomic changes have swung the world around. On the other hand, Mexican restaurants owned by Latinos have never turned down an Anglo. More than ever, all of us eat together, and we eat tacos and tortillas in abundance.

In this epilogue I have made a qualitative evaluation of the socioeconomic and political changes that have taken place in this generation. The substance of the information is based on my knowledge, formal and informal interviews, anecdotes, and local newspaper articles I have read on this topic. Throughout, I have focused on elements of integration between the two dominant groups. The results? Anglos and Latinos are working together to bring about greater integration compared to a generation ago. Opportunities have increased; Latinos have greater prospects for access to resources; and formal education among this group has exceeded expectations, something totally out of the question during my childhood. We continue to have command of our language and culture, and younger generation are growing toward a multicultural and multiracial society whether we like it or not. That stirs a portion of the white and nonwhite population across Texas and the nation.

Despite the many changes that have happened over the years, in some sectors of the Hispanic community, justice and equality have been evaded; poverty continues to dominate the lives of many people. That been said, I look forward to a new generation that offers a noble mission in bringing greater socioeconomic equality and justice. This whole book deals with the question of how unequally and unjustly we have been treated when compared to the white population. But over time change has made a difference.

Finally, in an interview with an Anglo historian, Dr. John Brockman, a person who reviewed this manuscript, we came to similar conclusions: Life is changing rapidly. Minorities are on the move, and there are no walls that will stop them.

Acknowledgments

I have many people to thank. Professionally, I can start back during my childhood when a poor blind man by the name of Abundio Chapa taught me how to read and write in Spanish. Much later, when I was stumbling to get a bachelor's degree at the Texas A&I University, Dr. George Coleson stood out among many good souls to make a difference in my life. Unlike many of my professors at that time, Dr. Coleson clearly understood the struggles of migrants and Mexican Americans and he fought for their rights. I also give thanks to a former graduate student from the University of Texas–El Paso, Dr. Sharon Navarro, now a professor of political science at the University of Texas–San Antonio, for her constant support over many years, including visiting my classes at UTSA. A wonderful scholar, her assistance and dedication come with love and sincerity. I thank Dr. John Brockman, a longtime, trustworthy friend who has always supported me in all my endeavors. Juanito's heart is sound, and he understands the dilemma of minorities. Thank you, John. My friend Dr. Rogelio Saenz has great appreciation for the many obstacles experienced by people of Mexican origin. This warrior has invited us consistently over time to his home in San Antonio. Rogelio loves to meet with old soldiers who fought for greater equality and justice for *la raza* (our people). Last but not least, thank you to the eighty architects of the first generation of Latinos in higher education who were willing to tell us their stories of their struggles and how they managed to become leaders in higher education. I will forever be proud of being part of this group.

Personally, I offer thanks to my parents, who, as immigrants, suffered at the hands of those who suppressed and condemned them because they were of Mexican origin. They knew of better things in life, and they raised seven children with love and care. My brothers and sisters were the best. They nurtured me and opened the gates for me to explore the world. I am thankful to my sister Oralia, who is not in a nursing home, and grateful to my wife Norma. She gives of her life and soul for the many crazy ideas I have. She does whatever it takes to have a good family. To Norma's parents and sister, who, like Norma, assisted me in every way possible, *gracias*! Norma and I have three kids, Marco Dante, Carlo Renato, and Ethel Minerva (Marco Dante lives with us, and he has been a great technical assistant for a person that learn limited technology at an older age). They have been the center of our life. We love them very much. I have four granddaughters: Carolina Antonia, Sofia Isabel, Valentina Minerva, and Ida Estelle. I am terribly pleased to be their grandpa. In every celebration that we have, and we have many, I remind them that my children (their parents) did a magnificent job in raising them, and that is why they are so special.

Endnotes

Note for the Preface

1. Roberto E. Villarreal, *First Generation of Latinos in Higher Education*, survey, 2003.

Notes for Chapter 1

1. David Montejano, *Anglos and Mexicans in the Making of Texas, 1836–1986* (Texas University Press, 1987).
2. Carrie Gibson, *El Norte: The Epic and Forgotten Story of Hispanic North America* (Atlantic Monthly Press, 2019), book flap
3. Tim Henderson, "More Hispanic Families Are Reaching the Middle Class," *Stateline*, https://stateline.org/2023/12/18/more-hispanic-families-are-reaching-the-middle-class/.
4. John Weber, *From South Texas to the Nation: The Exploitation of Mexican Labor in the Twentieth Century* (University of North Carolina Press, 2015), 27.

Notes for Chapter 3

1. Neil Foley, *The White Scourge: Mexicans, Blacks, and Poor Whites in Texas Cotton Culture* (University of California Press, 1997), 20.
2. Richard Parker, *Lone Star Nation: How Texas Will Transform America* (Pegasus Books, 2014), 82.
3. Jesús Chavarria, ed., "The 100 Influentials on Surviving in the New Millennium," *Hispanic Business* 19, no. 10 (October 1997).

Note for Chapter 4

1. Parker, *Lone Star Nation*, 7.

Note for Chapter 8

1. "UTEP Reasserts Prestigious R1 Research Status Under New Carnegie Classification Criteria," *UTEP Newsfeed*, February 26, 2025, https://www.utep.edu/newsfeed/2025/february/utep-reasserts-prestigious-r1-research-status-under-new-carnegie-classification-criteria.html.

Bibliography

Arreola, Daniel D. *Tejano South Texas: A Mexican American Cultural Province*. University of Texas Press, 2002.

Chavarria, Jesús, ed. "The 100 Influentials on Surviving in the New Millennium." *Hispanic Business* 19, no. 10 (October 1997).

Fernandez-Armesto, Felipe. *Our America: A Hispanic History of the United States*. W. W. Norton, 2014.

Foley, Neil. *The White Scourge: Mexicans, Blacks, and Poor Whites in Texas Cotton Culture*. University of California Press, 1997.

Galarza, Ernesto. *Barrio Boy*. University of Notre Dame Press, 2012.

Gibson, Carrie. *El Norte: The Epic and Forgotten Story of Hispanic North America*. Atlantic Monthly Press, 2019.

Goodwin, Robert. *America: The Epic of Spanish North America, 1493–1898*. Bloomsbury, 2019.

Limon, José. *Americo Paredes: Culture and Critique*. University of Texas Press, 2012.

Martinez, Monica Muñoz. *The Injustice Never Leaves You: Anti-Mexican Violence in Texas*. Harvard University Press, 2018.

Montejano, David. *Anglos and Mexicans in the Making of Texas, 1836–1986*. Texas University Press, 1987.

Paredes, Americo. *With His Pistol in His Hand: A Border Ballad and Its Hero*. Texas University Press, 1958.

Parker, Richard. *Lone Star Nation: How Texas Will Transform America*. Pegasus Books, 2014.

Rivera, Tomas. *Y No Se Lo Trago La Tierra*. Quinto Sol, 1971.

Villarreal, Roberto E. *Chicano Elites and Non-Elites: An Inquiry into Social and Political Change*. R&E, 1979.

Villarreal, Roberto E. *First Generation of Latinos in Higher Education*. Survey. 2003.

Villarreal, Roberto E., and Norma G. Hernandez, eds. *Latinos and Political Coalitions: Empowerment for the 1990s*. Greenwood Press, 1991.

Villarreal, Roberto E., Norma G. Hernandez, and Howard D. Neighbor, eds. *Latino Empowerment: Progress, Problems, and Prospects*. Greenwood Press, 1988.

Weber, John. *From South Texas to the Nation: The Exploitation of Mexican Labor in the Twentieth Century*. University of North Carolina Press, 2015.

Index